exotic
adornments

exotic adornments

18 Luxurious Beadwork Jewelry Projects

KELLY WIESE

INTERWEAVE.
interweave.com

contents

projects

introduction

When I started thinking about doing another book, I knew I wanted to approach it a little differently than my first two books. I wanted the projects to have a lush, exotic feel. Images of Bollywood dancers filled my head. Jewel tones, metallics, and crystals all came to mind. My work tends to have a romantic feel to it, and the projects in this book still do but with more glitz and glamour (I even named one of the projects Glitz and Glamour).

This is a project book, not a technique book. It will help if you are familiar with the basic beading stitches, but it isn't completely necessary. The projects are designed for advanced beginners to intermediate beaders. You can make the projects as is, or you can adapt them to suit your own style and taste. One of my favorite song lyrics is "life is a journey not a destination." This book is meant to be a beading journey. I encourage you to experiment, and most of all, have fun!

materials

There are so many wonderful materials available for use in beading these days. Listed here are some of my recommendations and preferences.

THREAD

I prefer to use a nylon beading thread, such as Nymo or One•G. It comes in a great variety of colors and is fairly inexpensive. FireLine is another good option. For the most part, it comes down to what you prefer to work with. FireLine is great when working with crystals, as it doesn't fray like nylon thread can. Nylon thread usually produces a softer piece of beadwork than FireLine does, so keep that in mind, too. I do like to use a thread conditioner such as Thread Heaven when I use nylon thread.

NEEDLES

I like to use a size 12 beading needle. Size 11 also works if you prefer a slightly larger eye. I use a lot of size 15 seed beads in my designs, so a smaller needle size is advised.

BEADS

I use Japanese seed beads in my designs, mostly in size 11 and size 15. I wish they made them even smaller than size 15. In my world, the smaller the better! I use colors from all three major manufacturers. There are differences in sizing with the different companies, so keep that in mind when choosing your color palette. Some will work a little better than others. I start by using colors I like and then make any adjustments if necessary as to the size and fit.

I used a lot of Swarovski crystals in the designs for this book. There is such a great selection of sizes and shapes available now that it is sometimes hard to decide what to use. I did use crystals that are easy to source, as I know it's frustrating not to be able to find the materials needed for a project.

I also used a lot of Swarovski and Czech glass pearls. I especially love the 2mm and 3mm sizes. Again, the smaller the better in my mind!

Left: Gold size 15 seed beads and jet crystals make an elegant, classic combination for the Swag Necklace (page 120). Here, bronze metallic iris beads complement the fuchsia and purple crystals and pearls of the Lotus Necklace (page 106).

techniques

This section covers the most common techniques used in the projects. A lot of the projects use multiple stitches, as I tend to mix and match stitches when I design.

↑ HALF-HITCH KNOT

To weave in threads, catch a thread between 2 beads, make a loop of thread, and pass through the loop. Pull the loop down on the thread between the beads. Make 2 or 3 half-hitch knots between beads before trimming the thread.

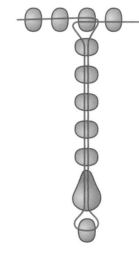

↑ FRINGE

Come out of a bead on the edge of the beadwork and string the desired number of beads, ending with a drop or larger bead plus 1 or 3 seed beads. Skip the seed beads and pass back up through the other beads to form a fringe.

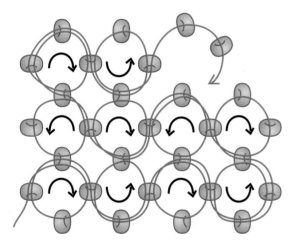

↑ RIGHT-ANGLE WEAVE (RAW)

String 4 beads and pass through the first 3 beads again. This forms the first unit. String 3 more beads and pass through the bead just exited and the first 2 of the 3 just strung. Continue until the desired number of units is added for the first row.

For the next row, exit from the top bead of the last unit. String 3 beads and pass through the last bead exited and the first bead of the 3 just strung. String 2 beads and pass through the next top bead of the previous row, the last bead exited in the previous unit, and the 2 beads just strung. Pass through the next top bead of the previous row. String 2 beads and pass through the last bead of the previous unit, the top bead just exited, and the first bead of the 2 just strung. Continue adding rows following these thread paths.

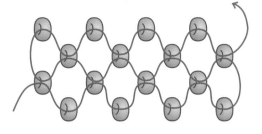

FLAT EVEN-COUNT PEYOTE STITCH

String an even number of beads. These will be the first 2 rows. Start the third row by stringing 1 bead and passing back through the second-to-last bead of the previous row. String 1 more bead, skip over the next bead of the previous row, and pass through the next bead. Repeat to the end of the row.

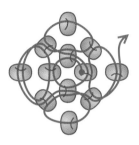

↑ CUBIC RIGHT-ANGLE WEAVE (CRAW)

String 4 beads. Pass through all the beads again and also pass through the first bead again. This is the base unit. I find it helps to think of CRAW units as having a base, 4 walls, and a ceiling.

Work CRAW by stringing 3 beads; pass through the bead the thread is exiting and also pass through the next bead in the base. This is the first wall.

String 2 beads and pass through the previous side bead and also pass through the bead of the base that the thread originally exited from and the first bead just added. This is the second wall. String 2 beads and pass through the next bead of the base. Pass up through the previous bead and also pass through the 2 beads just added, the next base bead, and up through the side bead of the first wall. This is the third wall.

String 1 bead and pass down through the side bead of the third wall and also pass through the base bead, then pass up through the side bead of the first wall and the bead just added. This is the fourth wall. Then pass through the top bead of each wall and also pass through the next top bead. This completes one cube, and the top is now the base for the next cube.

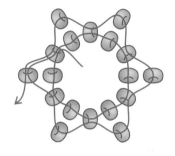

↑ CIRCULAR PEYOTE STITCH

String 12 beads and pass through them again, and also pass through the first bead again to form a circle. String 1 bead, skip over the next bead, and pass through the next one. Repeat for a total of 6 beads in this row. After adding the last bead, step up into the first bead added in this row to line up for the next row. Repeat for the desired number of rows.

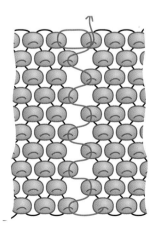

↑ ZIPPING PEYOTE STITCH

Connect 2 edges of peyote stitch by "zipping" the up beads on each side together like the teeth on a zipper.

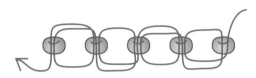

↑ LADDER STITCH

String 2 beads and pass through them again. They should sit side by side. String 1 bead and pass through the last bead added, and also pass through the bead just strung. Repeat, adding 1 bead at a time.

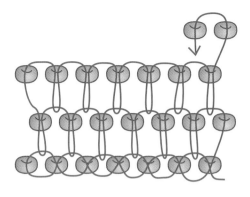

↑ BRICK STITCH

Working off a row of ladder stitch, string 2 beads and pass under the first thread between the beads. Pass back through the second bead. String 1 bead and pass under the next thread and back up the bead just added. Repeat. To decrease in a row, go under the second thread instead of the first thread when starting a row.

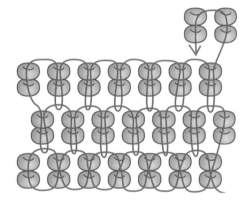

↑ 2-DROP BRICK STITCH

This is worked the same as regular brick stitch, but it is started with 4 beads and then 2 beads are added for each stitch.

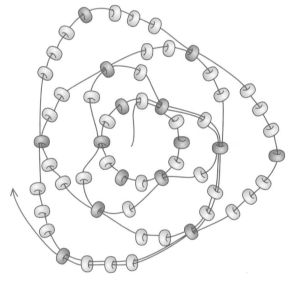

↑ CIRCULAR NETTING

String 12 beads and pass through all of them again. Also pass through the first bead again to form a circle. String 3 beads, skip over 3 beads of the circle, and pass through the next one. This creates a net. Repeat for a total of 6 nets. After adding the last net, step up through the first 2 beads of the first net to line up for the next row.

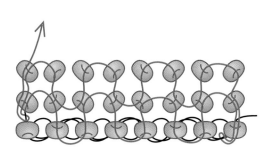

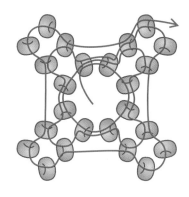

↑ FLAT HERRINGBONE STITCH

From a row of ladder stitch, string 2 beads and pass down through the second bead of the ladder stitch. Pass up the next bead of the ladder. Repeat to the end of the row. To start the next row, catch the thread on the ladder stitch and pass back up the last bead added. Keep adding rows by stringing 2 beads, passing down the next bead, and passing up the next bead.

↑ CIRCULAR HERRING-BONE STITCH

String 8 beads and pass through all of them again and also pass through the first 2 again to form a circle. String 2 beads and pass through the next 2 beads of the circle. Repeat three more times. Step up into the first bead added in this row. String 2 beads, pass down through the next bead, and pass up through the next bead. Repeat three more times. Step up into the first bead added in this row. Repeat for as many rows as desired.

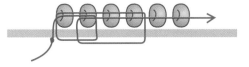

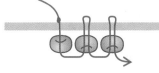

↑ BACKSTITCH FOR BEAD EMBROIDERY

Bring the thread up through the backing. String 2 beads and pass down at the end of them. Pass back up the backing, pass through the 2 beads, string 2 more beads, and pass down through the backing at the end. Pass back up the backing between the first and second bead and pass through the next 3 beads. Repeat, adding 2 beads and passing back through 3 beads.

↑ EDGING FOR BEAD EMBROIDERY

Come out of the Ultrasuede backing. String 2 beads and pass through the Ultrasuede about a bead's width over from where the thread originally exited. Pass back up through the second bead. String 1 bead and pass through the Ultrasuede about a bead's width over from where the thread originally exited, and pass back up the bead just added. Repeat around.

projects

I had so much fun designing the projects in this book. It was definitely a labor of love. I just hope you have as much fun making the projects as I had designing them.

Many of the projects are component based. So if some of the designs are a little over the top for you, the components can be used to make simpler versions of the projects. Think earrings, rings, and more—there are a lot of possibilities.

bead happy!

FINISHED SIZE

17" (43 cm)

SKILL LEVEL

Intermediate

MATERIALS

10 g purple gold metallic iris size 15° Japanese seed beads (A)

8 g midnight purple metallic luster size 15° Japanese seed beads (B)

14 g purple gold metallic iris size 11° Japanese seed beads (C)

12 jet 2mm round crystals (D)

14 tahitian 3mm glass pearls (E)

2 jet 3mm bicone crystals (F)

2 amethyst 12mm rivoli crystal stones

1 amethyst 27x18.5mm octagon crystal stone

1 jet 24mm crystal raindrop pendant

1 jet 8mm fire-polished bead

Size D nylon beading thread, brown

Thread conditioner

TOOLS

Size 12 beading needles

Scissors

TECHNIQUES YOU WILL USE

PEYOTE (PAGE 11)

NETTING (PAGE 12)

RIGHT-ANGLE WEAVE (PAGE 10)

bejeweled
PENDANT

I love the dramatic look of the large crystal octagon, and I wanted to design a piece that really showcased it. I kept the bezel fairly simple and added the smaller, more embellished crystals for a bit of flair. I also love the raindrop pendants and thought this was the perfect ending for the piece. If you don't want to make the spiral peyote rope, you could always string the pendant on a lovely silk ribbon.

SMALL CRYSTAL BEZEL

1 With 36" (91.5 cm) of thread, string 12A. Pass through all 12A again and also pass through the first A again. Leave a 6" (15 cm) tail (**Figure 1, green thread**).

2 Work circular peyote stitch by stringing 1A, skip over 1A from Step 1 and pass through the next 1A. Repeat for a total of 6A. Step up through the first A added in this row (**Figure 1, blue thread**).

3 Work circular peyote stitch with 1C for a total of 6C in this row. Step up through the first C added in this row. The beadwork is a little loose at this point, but don't pull it tight yet (**Figure 1, red thread**).

4 String 1A, 1C, and 1A and pass through the next C from Step 3. Repeat for a total of 6 sets. Step up through the first A and C added in this row (**Figure 2**).

5 String 2A, 1C, and 2A and pass through the middle C from the next set of beads from Step 4. Repeat for a total of 6 sets. After adding the last set, step up through the first 2A and the first C added in this row (**Figure 3**).

6 String 5A and pass through the middle C from the next set of beads from Step 5. Repeat for a total of 6 sets. Step up through the first 3A added in this row. Pull snug; the beadwork will start to cup up a little at this point (**Figure 4, blue thread**).

7 String 1A, 1C, and 1A and pass through the third A from the next set of 5A from Step 6. Repeat for a total of 6 sets. Insert 1 of the 12mm rivolis into the beadwork and pull snug (**Figure 4, red thread**). Reinforce this last row.

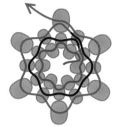

FIGURE 1

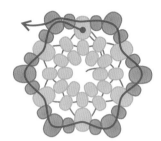

FIGURE 2

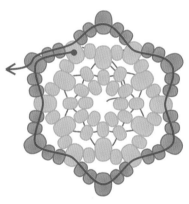

FIGURE 3

FIGURE 4

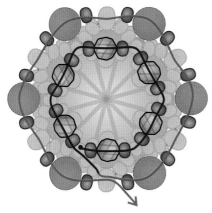

FIGURE 5

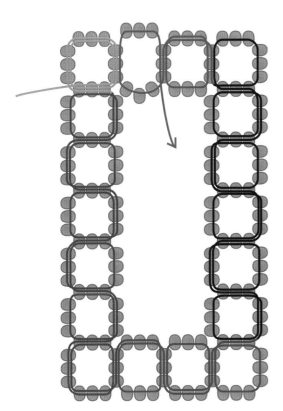

FIGURE 6

8 Weave the thread so that it is coming out of a third A from a set of 5A added in Step 6. String 1B, 1D, and 1B and pass through the third bead of the next set of 5A. Repeat for a total of 6 sets (**Figure 5, blue thread**).

9 Weave the thread so that it is coming out of a C from a set of beads from Step 5. String 1B, 1E, and 1B and pass through the next C of the next set of beads from Step 5. Repeat for a total of 6 sets (**Figure 5, red thread**). Weave in and tie off the tail thread.

10 Repeat Steps 1–9 to make another small crystal bezel.

LARGE OCTAGON BEZEL

11 With 72" (183 cm) of thread, string 12A. Pass through all 12A again and also go forward through the first 3A again. Leave a 6" (15 cm) tail (**Figure 6, orange thread**).

12 Work RAW with 12A per unit (3 beads per each side of the unit) by stringing 9A and passing through the first 3A of the previous unit. Also pass through the first 6A of the beads just added. Repeat for a total of 7 units. Pass through the next 3 beads of the unit just completed to begin the next side (**Figure 6, purple thread**).

13 Work 3 units with 12A from the side of the seventh unit from Step 12, for a total of 4 units on this side (**Figure 6, green thread**).

14 Work 6 units with 12A from the fourth unit added in Step 13, for a total of 7 units (**Figure 6, blue thread**).

15 Connect the end units on the rows of 7 units so that there are 4 units with 12A. It will require only 6A to connect the last unit to the previous units (3A for the top and 3A for the bottom of this unit) (**Figure 6, red thread**).

16 Weave the thread so that it is coming out of the middle bead of a side of a unit on the outside edge. String 3B and pass through the next middle bead of the side of the next unit. Repeat all the way around the outside of the beadwork, adding a total of 22 sets of 3B. At the corners, be sure to go through the middle bead on the top and side units. After adding the last set, step up through the first 2B of the first set added in this row (**Figure 7**).

17 String 3A and pass through the middle bead of the next set of 3B from Step 16. Repeat for a total of 22 sets of 3A. After adding the last set, step up through the first 2A of the first set added in this row (**Figure 8**).

18 String 1C and pass through the middle bead of the next set of 3A from Step 17. Repeat for a total of 22C. Step up into the first C added in this row. This row will start to cup up. Insert the octagon crystal into the beadwork, right side facing up, and pull the row snug. Adjust the beadwork if necessary so that the crystal is centered in the bezel (**Figure 9**, blue thread).

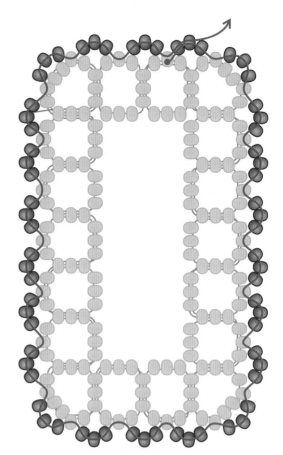

FIGURE 7

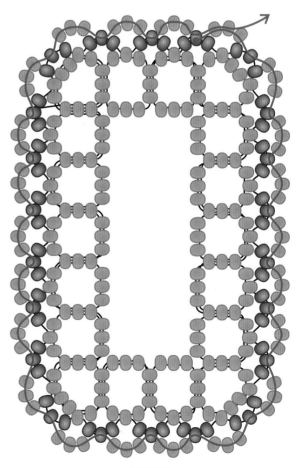

FIGURE 8

FIGURE 9

19 String 2A and pass through the next 1C from Step 18. Repeat for a total of 22 sets. Pull snug (**Figure 9, red thread**).

20 Weave the thread so that it is coming out of a middle bead of a set of 3A from Step 17. String 3A and pass through the middle bead of the next set of 3A from Step 17. Repeat for a total of 22 picots (**Figure 10**). Weave in and tie off the tail thread.

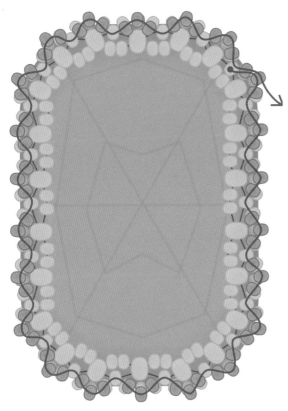

FIGURE 10

CONNECTIONS, BAIL, AND DROP

21 Weave the thread on the large octagon bezel so that it is coming out of a bead from Step 16 or 17 on a short side that is closest to the middle. Pass through a C from Step 5 on a small bezel, then pass through the middle bead on the octagon bezel, then through C again (**Figure 11**).

22 Then pass through the next 1B and 1E on the small bezel. String 1C and pass through a bead on the octagon bezel that is closest to the 1E just exited. Then weave over to the other side of the middle connection and repeat. Make sure the connection is centered (**Figure 12**).

23 Repeat the connection with the other small bezel on the other short end of the octagon bezel.

24 For the bail, weave a thread on one of the small bezels so that it is coming out of the 1B from Step 9 that is directly across from the connection of the bezels. String 1A and pass through the next 1B on the bezel.

25 String 1A and pass back through the A added in Step 24. String 1A and catch the thread between the B and E and then pass back through the A just added (**Figure 13**). This is flat odd-count peyote. Keep adding rows until there are 22A on each side.

26 Fold the peyote strip in half and pass through the beads of the first row and the last row to zip the ends together (**Figure 14, blue thread**). Weave the thread so that it is coming out of the first A of the peyote strip. String 3B, go down the next A of the strip, and come up the next A. Repeat adding picots to the edge of the strip (**Figure 14, red thread**). Then weave over to the other side and repeat.

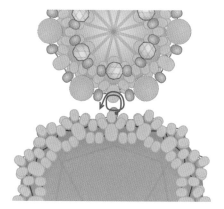

FIGURE 11

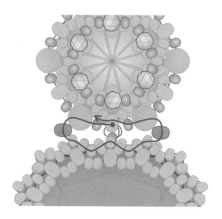

FIGURE 12

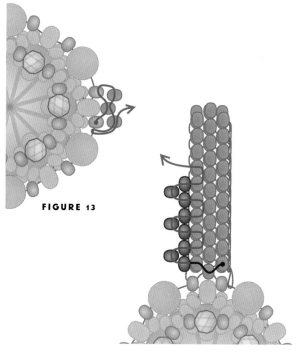

FIGURE 13

FIGURE 14

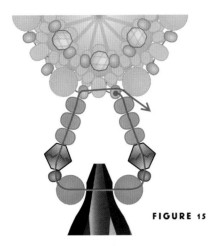

FIGURE 15

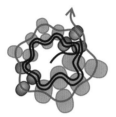

FIGURE 16

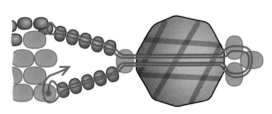

FIGURE 17

FIGURE 18

27 On the other small bezel, weave the thread so that it is coming out of one of the 1B directly across from the connection of the bezels. String 3C, 1F, 1B, 1E, the raindrop crystal, 1E, 1B, 1F, and 3C and pass through the 1B and 1C next to the one previously exited (**Figure 15**).

SPIRAL ROPE

28 With 72" (183 cm) of thread, string 2B, 4A, 2B, and 4C. Pass through all the beads again and also pass through the first B. Leave a 12" (30.5 cm) tail (**Figure 16, blue thread**).

29 Work circular peyote stitch by stringing 1B, skipping over the next 1B, and passing through the next 1A of the original circle. Continue around the circle, stringing the same size and color bead that the thread is exiting from. This makes the spiral pattern in the rope. Step up into the first bead added in this row (**Figure 16, red thread**).

30 Keep working circular peyote stitch following Step 29. Pull each row snug and make sure to do the step up at the end of each row. The peyote rope should be about 16" (40.5 cm) long.

31 With the tail thread left earlier, string 5B, 1C, the 8mm fire-polished bead, and 3C. Skip the 3C and pass back through the 8mm bead and the next 1C. String 5B and pass through a bead on the last row of the rope across from the first 5B. Reinforce (**Figure 17**).

32 On the other end of the rope, string 5B, 1C, and enough B to fit comfortably but snugly around the 8mm bead. Then pass back through the 1C. String 5B and pass through a bead on the last row of the rope across from the first 5B. Reinforce (**Figure 18**).

FINISHED SIZE

16½" (42 cm)

SKILL LEVEL

Advanced

MATERIALS

10 g permanent gold galvanized size 15° Japanese seed beads (A)

40 g gold electroplate size 11° Japanese seed beads (B)

12 g brass olivine metallic iris size 11° Japanese seed beads (C)

40 crystal iridescent green 39ss crystal rivolis (D)

3 medium 9x6mm vitrail drop beads

1 medium 6mm vitrail round bead

Size D nylon beading thread, gold

Thread conditioner

TOOLS

Size 12 beading needles

Scissors

TECHNIQUES YOU WILL USE

CUBIC RIGHT-ANGLE WEAVE (PAGE 11)

FRINGE (PAGE 10)

NETTING (PAGE 12)

captured crystals
CHOKER

I love the look of chokers and wanted to make one with an elegant touch. This particular design does not have to be worn tightly around the neck; it can be worn a little looser, as it has a fairly substantial band. A shorter version of the band would make a great bracelet.

CRAW ROPE

1 With 72" (183 cm) of thread, string 4B. Pass through all the beads again and pass through the first B again (**Figure 1, blue thread**). Leave a 12" (30.5 cm) tail. This will be the base of the rope. I find it helps to think of CRAW units as having a base, 4 walls, and a ceiling.

2 Work CRAW by stringing 3B; pass through the B the thread is exiting from and also pass through the next B in the base. This is the first wall (**Figure 1, red thread**).

3 String 2B and pass through the side B from Step 2 and also pass through the B of the base that thread originally exited from and the first B added in this step. This is the second wall (**Figure 2**).

4 String 2B and pass through the next B of the base. Pass up through the B from Step 3 and also pass through the 2B just added, the next base bead, and up through the side B of the first wall. This is the third wall (**Figure 3**).

5 String 1B and pass down through the side bead of the third wall and also pass through the base bead, pass up through the side bead of the first wall, and the top 1B of the first wall (**Figure 4**). This is the fourth wall. Then pass through the top bead of each wall and also pass through the next top bead (**Figure 5**). Pull snug to firm up the cube shape (**Figure 6**). This completes one cube, and the top is now the base for the next cube.

6 Keep working CRAW following Steps 2–5 until the rope is about 15½" (39.5 cm) long. Then work 5 cubes off the side wall so that there are 6 cubes. This is the end of the choker. Then work CRAW off the side wall of the sixth cube until it is as long as the first rope (**Figure 7**). Set this aside.

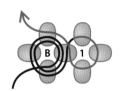
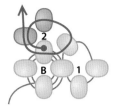

FIGURE 1   **FIGURE 2**

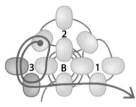
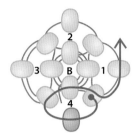

FIGURE 3

FIGURE 4

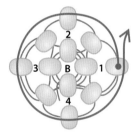

FIGURE 5

FIGURE 6

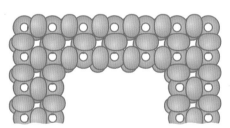

FIGURE 7

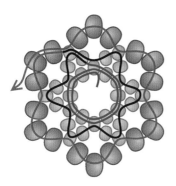

FIGURE 8

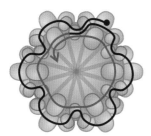

FIGURE 9

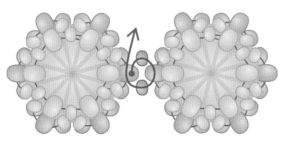

FIGURE 10

SMALL CRYSTAL BEZELS

7 With 36" (91.5 cm) of thread, string 12A and pass through all the beads again, and also go through the first A again. Leave a 6" (15 cm) tail (**Figure 8, green thread**).

8 String 3A, skip over the next A from the original circle, and go through the next A. Repeat for a total of 6 nets. Step up through the first 2A added in this row (**Figure 8, blue thread**).

9 String 3C and then pass through the middle bead of the next set of 3A from Step 8. Repeat for a total of 6 nets. Step up through the first 2C added in this row (**Figure 8, red thread**).

10 String 3A and then pass through the middle bead of the next set of 3C from Step 9. Repeat for a total of 6 nets. Step up through the first 2A added in this row. This row will start to cup a little (**Figure 9, blue thread**).

11 Place 1 of the rivolis into the beadwork, right side facing up. String 1B and pass through the middle bead of the next set of 3A from Step 10. Repeat for a total of 6B (**Figure 9, red thread**). Pull snug and reinforce this row. Weave in and tie off the tail thread.

12 Make 39 more small crystal bezels following Steps 7–11.

CONNECTIONS FOR THE BAND AND PENDANT

13 Weave a thread on a small bezel so that it is coming out of a middle C from a set of 3C from Step 9. String 1A and pass through a middle C from a set of 3C on another small bezel. String 1A and pass through the C the thread originally exited from (**Figure 10**). Reinforce this connection one more time. This is how all the crystals are connected together for the choker.

14 Connect a total of 29 of the crystal bezels together following Step 13. Connect them at the middle Cs that are directly across from each other so that they make a straight line. Weave in and tie off the threads as you connect the bezels.

15 Connect 6 of the crystal bezels together to form a circle, following Step 13 (**Figure 11, blue thread**). Then connect a seventh bezel in the middle of the circle. It will be connected at all 6 of the middle C beads from Step 9 (**Figure 11, red thread**).

16 Connect 3 of the crystal bezels together to form a triangle following Step 13 (**Figure 12**).

17 Weave the thread on the triangle so that it is coming out of a middle C next to the connection of 2 of the bezels that make up the triangle. It should be coming out on the far side of the C. String 3B and pass through the middle C on the circle of bezels. String 3C and pass through the corresponding C of the next bezel. Reinforce the connection of the circle of bezels to the triangle of bezels (**Figure 13**).

18 Weave a thread on the single bezel of the triangle so that it is coming out the second C away from the connection. It should be coming out on the far side of the C. String 5B, 1 drop bead, 1B, 1 drop bead, 1B, 1 drop bead, and 4B. Skip 3B and go back up the next B, the drop beads, and 1B between them and come out of the 1B above the first drop bead. String 4B and go through the middle C of the next C on the bottom bezel of the triangle (**Figure 14**). Set the pendant aside for now.

FIGURE 11

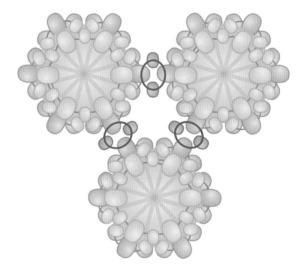

FIGURE 12

FIGURE 13

FIGURE 14

19 Weave a new 60" (152.5 cm) thread into the CRAW rope at the end with the 6 cubes. Come out of the B on the inside top of the second cube of the rope (**Figure 15, blue thread**).

20 Pass through a middle C from Step 9 on the side of the strand of connected bezels and then pass through the next B on the rope (it will be the next inside B of the next cube). String 1C and pass through the next B of the rope. Pass through the next C on the same bezel. Pass through the next B of the rope. String 1C and pass through the next B of the rope. Pass through the next C of the next bezel. Be sure to pull snug so that the beads fit together like a zipper (**Figure 15, red thread**).

21 Follow Step 20 to connect all the bezels to the rope. When you get to the end of the bezels, you may need to add or remove some of the beads of the rope. There should be 1 more cube after the last bezel is connected at the last C.

22 Repeat Steps 19–21 on the other side of the rope and the other side of the strand of bezels. Make sure that this side also has 1 more cube after the last bezel is connected at the last C. The ropes need to be the same length. Then add 4 cubes with CRAW to the sides of the ropes to connect them. There should be 6 cubes at the end.

23 Figure 16 illustrates the connection of the pendant to the band. It is connected at the fourteenth, fifteenth, and fourteenth bezels, counting in from each end. There are 6B added on the side connections and 1A added on each side of the center connection.

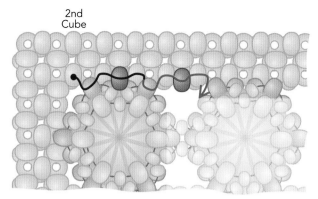

2nd Cube

FIGURE 15

FIGURE 16

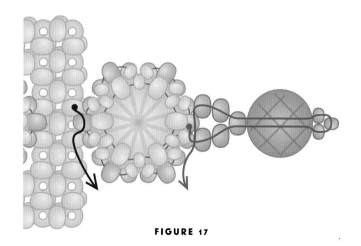

FIGURE 17

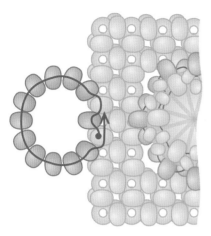

FIGURE 18

CLASP BEAD AND LOOP

24 Weave a thread so that it is coming out the side B of the third cube at the end of the band. Then pass through the middle C of the last bezel on the row from Step 9 with 3C **(Figure 17, blue thread)**. Pass through the next B. Reinforce. Weave over to the C across from the connection. String 3B, 1 6mm bead, and 3A. Skip the 3A and pass back through the 6mm bead and the next B. String 2B and pass through the C the thread originally exited from **(Figure 17, red thread)**. Reinforce.

25 On the other end of the band, weave a thread so that it is coming out of the side B of the third cube at the end of the band. String 1B and go through the next B on the band. String enough B to fit comfortably but snugly around the 6mm bead. Then pass through the B on the band that the thread started in **(Figure 18)**. Reinforce.

mythril
BRACELET

FINISHED SIZE

7" (18 cm)

SKILL LEVEL

Intermediate

MATERIALS

8 g palladium electroplate size
15° Japanese seed beads (A)

16 g dark silver electroplate size
11° Japanese seed beads (B)

98 crystal silver night 3mm
crystal bicones (C)

48 silver 3mm glass pearls (D)

4 silver 4mm glass pearls

Size D nylon beading thread, gray

Thread conditioner

TOOLS

Size 12 beading needles

Scissors

**TECHNIQUES
YOU WILL USE**

CHAIN VARIATION

This particular bracelet is one of my all-time favorites. It feels like a luxurious fabric on your arm. It is slinky, soft, and very versatile. It can be worn with jeans or with a little black dress. I really debated about what type of closure to use for it. I ended up going with the four small loop and beads and was quite happy with how it looks when worn.

CHAINS

1 With 72" (183 cm) of thread, string 5B and tie them into a circle. Leave a 12" (30.5 cm) tail.

2 String 5B and pass up through the second B of the original circle and also pass up through the second B of the 5B just added (**Figure 1**). Pull snug.

3 String 5B and pass up through the second bead from where the thread is exiting. Also pass up through the second B of the 5B just added (**Figure 2**). Pull snug.

4 **Figure 3** illustrates how the chain should look in progress. There should be beads sticking out on both sides. One side of the chain will always have 1 less bead. Repeat Step 3 until the chain has 50 beads sticking out on one side and 49 beads sticking out on the other side.

5 The tail thread left earlier should be coming out of the 2B sticking out at the end of the chain. String 3A, 1B, a 4mm pearl, and 3A. Skip the 3A and pass back through the 4mm pearl and the 1B. String 3A and pass through the B next to the one the thread originally exited from (**Figure 4**). Reinforce. Weave in and tie off the remaining tail thread.

6 Repeat Steps 1–5 to make another chain that has 50B on one side and 49 on the other side.

7 Repeat Steps 1–5 to make 2 more chains that have 49B on one side and 48 on the other side. There are a total of 4 chains in the bracelet.

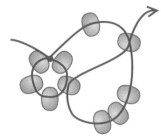

FIGURE 1

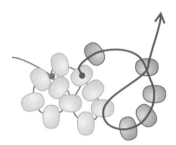

FIGURE 2

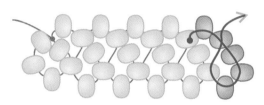

FIGURE 3

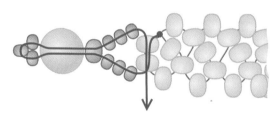

FIGURE 4

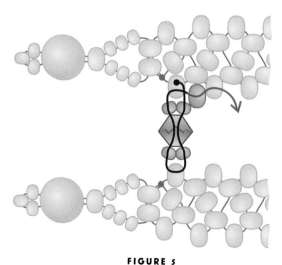

FIGURE 5

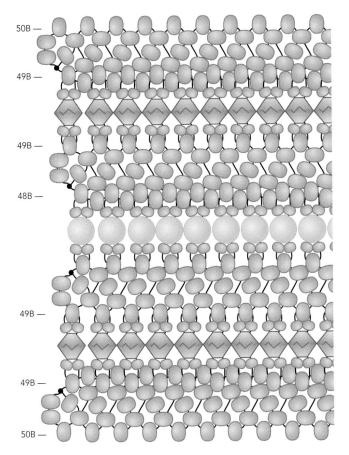

50B —
49B —

49B —

48B —

49B —

49B —

50B —

FIGURE 6

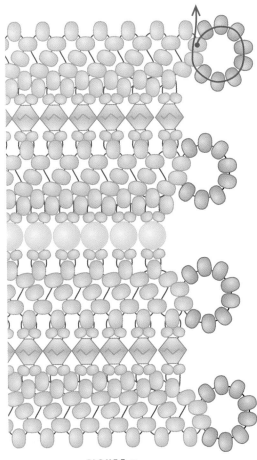

FIGURE 7

CONNECTIONS

8 Weave a new 72" (183 cm) thread so that it is coming out of the first B sticking out on the side with 49B on a chain with 50 and 49B on the sides. String 1A, 1C, and 1A and pass through the first B sticking out on a chain with 49 and 48B on the side with 49B. String 1A and pass back through the C. String 1A and pass through the B the thread originally exited (**Figure 5, blue thread**).

9 String 1B and pass through the next B on the side of the chain (**Figure 5, red thread**).

10 Continue connecting the 2 chains together following Steps 8–9 until there are 49 connections between the chains.

11 Connect the remaining chains following Steps 8–9. The center connection of the chains with 48B on each side is done in the same way, except use a D instead of a C. **Figure 6** illustrates the proper order for the chain and connections.

12 After the chains are all connected, weave a thread on the end of the first chain so that it is coming out of one of the 2B at the end. String enough B to fit comfortably but snugly around the 4mm pearl. Pass through the B next to the one the thread originally exited. Reinforce. Repeat on all 4 chains (**Figure 7**).

all squared away
BRACELET

FINISHED SIZE

7½" (19 cm)

SKILL LEVEL

Intermediate

MATERIALS

4 g gold electroplate size 15°
Japanese seed beads (A)

9 g gold bronze metallic iris size
11° Japanese seed beads (B)

5 g gold electroplate size 11°
Japanese seed beads (C)

124 crystal golden shadow 2mm
round crystals (D)

120 amethyst 3mm
bicone crystals (E)

40 crystal 3mm golden shadow
bicone crystals (F)

2 gold pearl 4mm round
glass beads (G)

Size D nylon beading thread, tan

Thread conditioner

TOOLS

Size 12 beading needles

Scissors

TECHNIQUES YOU'LL USE

PEYOTE (PAGE 11)

RIGHT-ANGLE WEAVE
(PAGE 10)

I designed this bracelet to showcase the right-angle weave (RAW) stitch. I used a lot of crystals so it would catch the light with each movement of the wrist. The way the smaller crystal squares attach to the larger open squares gives this piece its dimension.

OPEN SQUARES

1 Use 72" (183 cm) of thread and 22B (each unit has 4B) to make a strip of right-angle weave (RAW) that is 7 units long. End with the thread coming out of a side B on the last unit (**Figure 1, purple thread**).

2 Use 18B to work another strip of right-angle weave that is 6 units off of the first side. End with the thread coming out of the inside B of the last unit added (**Figure 1, green thread**).

3 Use 18B to work another strip of right-angle weave that is 6 units off of the second side. End with the thread coming out of the inside B of the last unit added (**Figure 1, blue thread**).

4 Use 12B to work a strip of right-angle weave 4 units long off of the third side. Then string 1B and pass through the inside B of the first unit in side one; string 1B and pass through the nearest B of the final unit added on this side. End with the thread coming out of a B on the outside edge. This is the base of the square (**Figure 1, red thread**).

5 Work a row of peyote stitch by stringing 1C and passing through the next outer B on the RAW square; repeat for a total of 28C. Step up through the first C added in this round (**Figure 2, green thread**).

6 Work another row of peyote by stringing 1B and passing through the next C from Step 5; repeat for a total of 28B. Weave through the beads and come out of an inside B from the RAW square (**Figure 2, blue thread**).

7 String 1C and pass through the next inside B on the RAW square; repeat for a total of 20C. Weave in and tie off the tail thread. Leave the working thread attached for now (**Figure 2, red thread**).

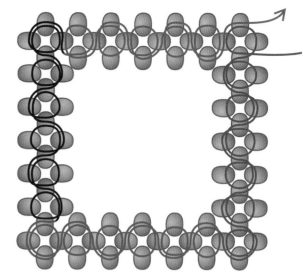

FIGURE 1

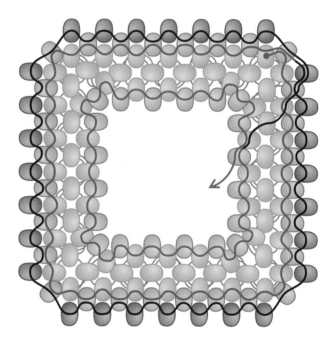

FIGURE 2

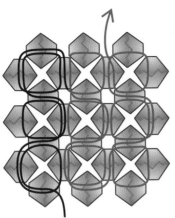

FIGURE 3

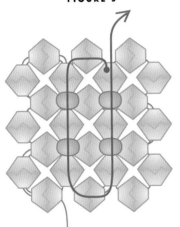

FIGURE 4

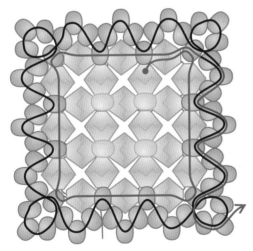

FIGURE 5

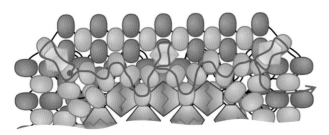

FIGURE 6

CRYSTAL SQUARES

8 Use 48" (122 cm) of thread and 10E to work a row of right-angle weave 3 units long (**Figure 3, blue thread**).

9 Add 2 more rows of right-angle weave with 14E (**Figure 3, red thread**).

10 Weave the thread so that it is coming out of a side E on the inside of an end unit. String 1C and go through the next E. String 1C and go through the next E. Weave through the end bead of the unit and repeat on the next side E of the next units (**Figure 4**).

11 Weave the working thread so that it is coming out of an outside E. String 1C and pass through the next E. Repeat all the way around, adding a total of 12C. Step up into the first C added in this row (**Figure 5, green thread**).

12 String 3A and pass through the next C; repeat around. At the corners, string 3A and pass back through the A the thread exited from to create a picot (**Figure 5, blue thread**). Weave in and tie off the tail thread. Weave the working thread so that it is coming out of a middle A of a picot at a corner (**Figure 5, red thread**).

CONNECTING THE SQUARES

13 With the thread on the crystal square, string 1F and pass through the C from Step 5 of the base square that is at the corner. Pass back through the F and pass through the middle A of the picot. Weave over to the middle A of the middle set of 3A from Step 12 on the side of the square. String 1F and pass through the fourth top B of the RAW unit on the base square. Pass back through the F and pass through the A; repeat to add a total of 8F that connect the crystal square to the base square (**Figure 6**).

14 Make 4 more layered squares following Steps 1–13.

OTHER CONNECTIONS

15 There are 7B on each side of the base square. Weave a thread on the base square so that it is coming out of an end B on a side. Use 8B and RAW to connect the 7B on the side of one square to the 7B on the side of another square (**Figure 7**).

16 Weave the thread so that it is coming out of an end B of the 7B on a side of a base square. String 1D and pass through the next B; repeat until you have added 6D. Weave through the end B and the next side B and repeat until you have added 6 more D (**Figure 8**).

17 Repeat Steps 15–16 to connect all 5 of the layered squares.

TOGGLE SQUARE

18 Follow Steps 1–7 to create a base square. After completing Step 7, work another row of peyote with 20A (**Figure 9, green thread**).

19 Weave the working thread so that it is coming out of a B on the inside edge (a B that is part of the RAW). String 1D and pass through the next B on the inside edge; repeat, adding a total of 20D. End with the thread coming out of the first D added in this row (**Figure 9, blue thread**).

20 String 1A and pass through the next D; repeat, adding a total of 20A (**Figure 9, red thread**).

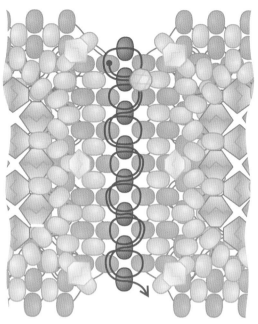

FIGURE 7

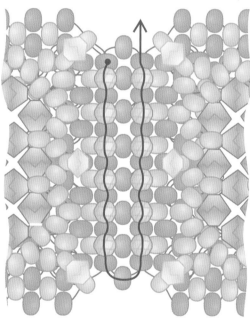

FIGURE 8

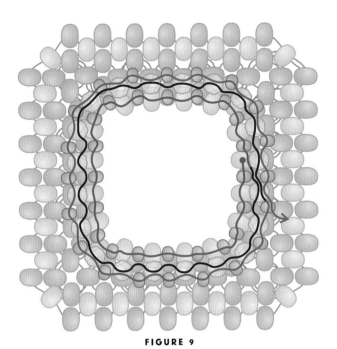

FIGURE 9

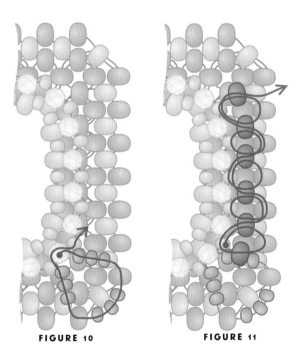

FIGURE 10   **FIGURE 11**

21 Weave the thread so that it is coming out of a D at the corner of the square. String 3A and pass through the B at the outside corner. String 3A and pass through the next B at the outside corner; string 3A and pass through the D the thread started in and also pass through the next A that was added in Step 20 (**Figure 10**).

22 Using 5A added in Step 20 and the 5B on the outside edge of the square, work RAW on the top side of the square adding 6B to make the units (**Figure 11**).

23 At the corner, repeat Step 21 and then repeat Step 22 down the next side. Repeat for the third corner and the third side and fourth corner. Do not work RAW on the last (fourth) side. Follow Steps 15–16 to connect the toggle square to the other squares on the last side.

TOGGLE BAR

24 Use 48" (122 cm) of thread and 10B to work a row of RAW 3 units long (**Figure 12, blue thread**).

25 Add 11 more rows of RAW with B (**Figure 12, red thread**).

26 Fold the piece and use RAW with 13B to connect the beadwork and turn it into a tube shape. Then weave the thread so that it is coming out of a B going toward the beadwork (**Figure 13**).

27 String 1D and pass through the next B; repeat, adding a total of 11D down one side of the toggle bar and 11D up the next side (**Figure 14**). Repeat on the other 2 sides, adding a total of 44D to the toggle bar. Then weave the thread to one of the 4B at the end of the bar. String 1G and 3C; pass back through the 1G and reinforce in the 4B at the end of the bar (**Figure 15, red thread**). Repeat on the other end. Then weave the thread to the seventh B on one side of the bar, counting from one end. String 12B and pass through the fourth B at the end of the bracelet on the outside of the last layered square. String 12B and pass through the sixth B, the next D, and the next B (**Figure 15, blue thread**).

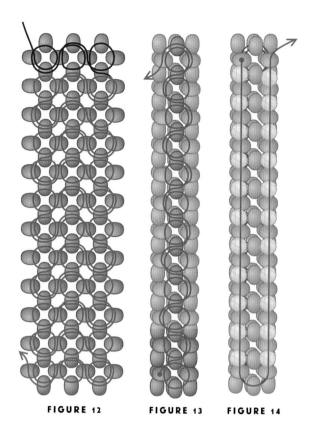

FIGURE 12   **FIGURE 13**   **FIGURE 14**

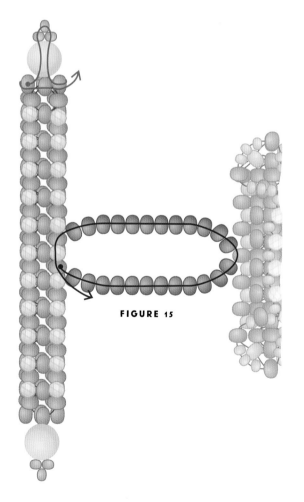

FIGURE 15

FINISHED SIZE

1½" × 2" (3.8 x 5 cm)

SKILL LEVEL

Advanced Beginner

MATERIALS

3 g light aqua/bronze-lined size 15° Japanese seed beads (A)

2 g gold bronze metallic size 15° Japanese seed beads (B)

3 g gold bronze metallic size 11° Japanese seed beads (C)

48 shiny turquoise blue 2mm glass pearls (D)

12 blue zircon 3mm crystal bicones (E)

2 light turquoise 11x5.5mm crystal drops

2 light turquoise 12mm rivoli crystal stones

1 pair gold ear wires

Nylon beading thread, turquoise

Thread conditioner

TOOLS

Size 12 beading needles

Scissors

TECHNIQUES YOU WILL USE

FRINGE (PAGE 10)

NETTING (PAGE 12)

PEYOTE (PAGE 11)

celestial
EARRINGS

I was playing around with some rivolis, trying different bezels, and I came up with this design that looks like a star on top of the rivoli. Then I wanted to add something a little different to it, and I came up with the half circle, which reminded me of a moon. Thus the Celestial Earrings were born. It is a fun, lightweight design that works up fairly quickly.

STAR BEZELS

1 With 72" (183 cm) of thread, string 12A. Pass through all 12A again and also pass through the first A again.

2 Work a row of peyote stitch with 6A. Step up into the first A added in this row (**Figure 1, blue thread**).

3 Work a row of peyote stitch with 6C. Step up into the first C added in this row (**Figure 1, red thread**).

4 String 3C and pass through the next C from Step 3. Repeat for a total of 6 sets of 3C. Step up into the first 2C of the first 3 added in this row (**Figure 2, blue thread**).

5 String 5A and pass through the middle C from the next set of 3C from Step 4. Repeat for a total of 6 sets of 5A. Step up into the first 3A of the first 5A added in this row (**Figure 2, red thread**).

6 String 7A and pass through the middle A from the next set of 5A from Step 5. Repeat for a total of 6 sets of 7A. Step up into the first 4A of the first 7A added in this row (**Figure 3, blue thread**).

7 String 1C and pass through the middle A from the next set of 7A from Step 6. Repeat for a total of 6C. Insert 1 of the 12mm rivolis into the beadwork, right side facing up. Pull the beadwork snug and reinforce this row (**Figure 3, red thread**).

8 Weave the thread so that it is coming out of the middle A of a set of 5A from Step 5. String 1B, 1E, and 1B. Pass through the next middle A of the next set of 5A. Repeat for a total of 6 sets. Step up into the first 1B, 1E, and 1B added in this row (**Figure 4, blue thread**).

9 String 1B, 1D, and 1B and pass through the next 1B, 1E, and B added in Step 8. Repeat for a total of 6 sets (**Figure 4, red thread**).

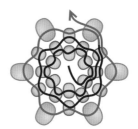

FIGURE 1

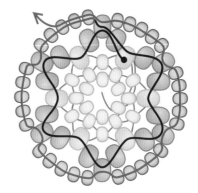

FIGURE 2

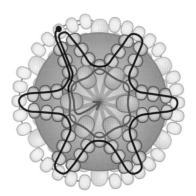

FIGURE 3

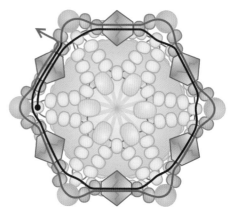

FIGURE 4

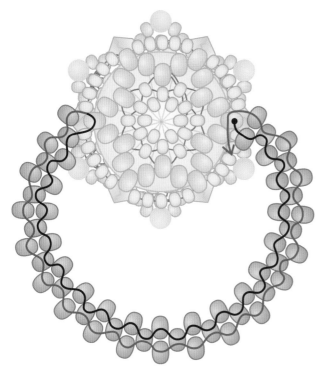

FIGURE 5

FIGURE 6

PEYOTE LOOP

10 Weave the thread so that it is coming out of a middle C from a set of 3C from Step 4. Then string 36C and pass through the middle C of the third set, counting away from where the thread originally exited (**Figure 5, blue thread**).

11 String 1C and pass back through the thirty-sixth C. Work a row of peyote with 19C. To anchor the last (nineteenth) C, pass through the middle C from Step 4 (**Figure 5, red thread**).

12 Weave the thread around and come out of the nineteenth C. String 1D and pass through the next C from Step 11. Repeat for a total of 18D (**Figure 6, blue thread**).

13 String 1C and pass back through the eighteenth D added in Step 12. Work a row of peyote with 19C. To anchor the last (nineteenth) C, catch the thread at the end of the row and pass back through the nineteenth C, and also pass back through the next D and C (**Figure 6, red thread**).

14 String 3A and pass through the next C from Step 13. String 2A and pass through the next C. Keep repeating, alternating between adding 3A and 2A until you have 8 sets. String 8B, 1 of the drop beads, and 8B. Pass through the C the thread originally exited from. This will make a small loop fringe. String 2A and pass through the next C. String 3A and pass through the next C. Repeat until you have added 8 sets on this side of the circle. After adding the last set, also pass through the next D and C (**Figure 7**).

15 String 2C and pass through the first C of the same 3C that the peyote loop is attached to. Weave through the beads to the other side and come out of the first C of the other set of 3C that the peyote loop is attached to. String 2C and pass through the C at the end of the peyote loop (**Figure 8**).

16 Weave the thread and come out of the D at the top of the bezel, above the peyote loop. String 8B and pass through the D the thread originally exited from (**Figure 9**). Reinforce. Add an ear wire to the loop.

17 Repeat Steps 1–16 to make another earring.

tip

If you want to stiffen the peyote loops a little, brush a light coat of clear floor polish on them and let them dry. It won't hurt the finish on the beads, and it will stiffen the beadwork.

FIGURE 7

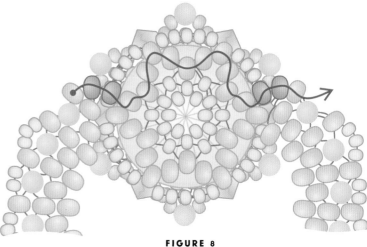

FIGURE 8

FIGURE 9

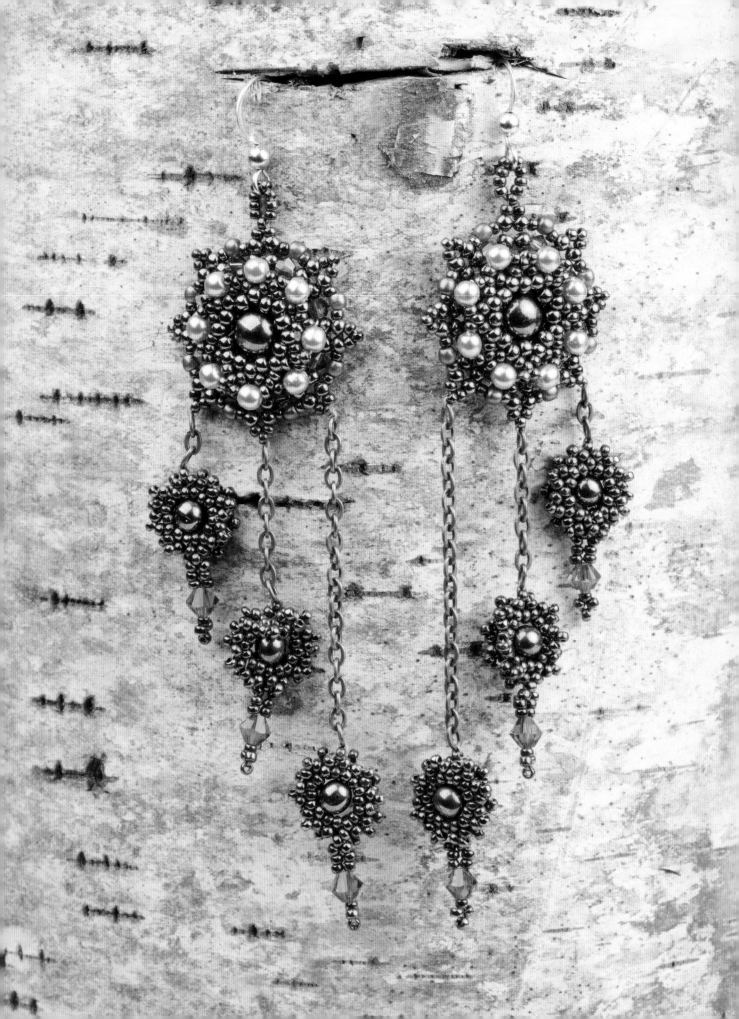

1" x 4" (2.5 x 10 cm)

SKILL LEVEL

Intermediate

MATERIALS

3 g bronze metallic iris size 15°
Japanese seed beads (A)

3 g gold bronze metallic size 11°
Japanese seed beads (B)

16 teal 2mm glass pearls (C)

16 blue zircon 3mm
bicone crystals (D)

16 gold 3 mm glass pearls (E)

6 light bronze 4mm druks (F)

6 blue zircon 4mm
bicone crystals (G)

2 light bronze 6mm druks (H)

8" (20.5 cm) antiqued brass
2mm flat cable chain

1 pair gold ear wires

Size D nylon beading thread,
brown

Thread conditioner

TOOLS

Size 12 beading needles

Scissors

**TECHNIQUES
YOU WILL USE**

HERRINGBONE (PAGE 13)

NETTING (PAGE 12)

PEYOTE (PAGE 11)

star-struck
EARRINGS

I am a big fan of statement earrings. I especially like earrings with long fringe that moves when I do. These earrings are very lightweight and have great movement. You can always make the chain sections a little shorter if they are too long for you.

TOP COMPONENT

1 Use 60" (152.5 cm) of thread to string 1H and 8B, leaving a 6" (15 cm) tail. Pass through the H. String 8B and pass through the H again. Then pass through all 16B again to pull them together around the 1H. Also go through a few more B to close any gaps (**Figure 1**).

2 String 1B and pass through the B the thread is exiting from in Step 1 and also go forward through the next B from Step 1. Keep repeating until you have gone all the way around the circle, adding a total of 16B. End with the thread coming out of a B from this row (**Figure 2**).

3 Pass through all the B from the Step 2 row and pull snug. This will make the row from Step 2 stack on top of row 1 from Step 1 (**Figure 3**).

4 String 3A, skip over the next B, and go through the next one. Repeat for a total of 8 sets of 3A. After adding the last set of 3A, step up into the first 2A of the first point added in this row (**Figure 4**).

5 String 1A, 1E, and 1A and then pass through the middle A of the next set of 3A from Step 4. Repeat for a total of 8 sets. This is the last row for the top layer of the component, so there is no step up (**Figure 5**). Weave in and tie off the tail thread.

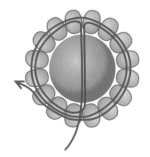

FIGURE 1

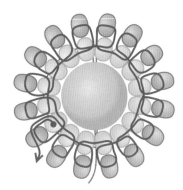

FIGURE 2

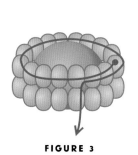

FIGURE 3

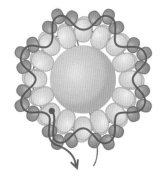

FIGURE 4

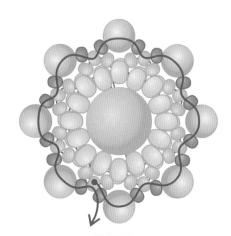

FIGURE 5

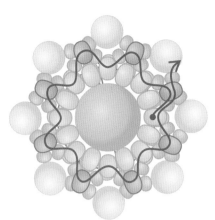

FIGURE 6

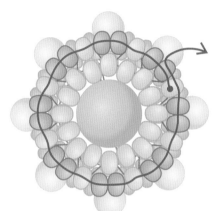

FIGURE 7

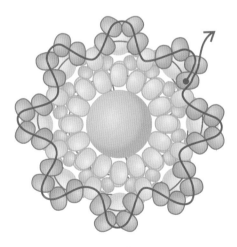

FIGURE 8

6 Weave down to the other row of B on the other side. String 1B, skip over the next B, and pass through the next B. Repeat for a total of 8B. Step up into the first B of this row (**Figure 6**).

7 String 2B and pass through the next B from Step 6. Repeat for a total of 8 sets. Step up into the first B of the first set of 2B added in this row (**Figure 7**).

8 String 2B and pass down through the next B. Also pass up through the first B of the next set from Step 7 (herringbone stitch). Repeat until you have added 16 sets of 2B. After adding the last set, step up into the first B of the first set added in this row (**Figure 8**).

9 String 2B and pass down through the next B. Then string 1D and pass up through the first B of the next set. Repeat for a total of 8 sets. After adding the last set, step up into the first B of the first set added in this row (**Figure 9**).

10 String 3A and pass down the next B. String 1A, 1C, and 1A and pass up through the next B of the next set. Repeat for a total of 8 sets. After adding the last set, step up through the first 2A of a set of 3A over a herringbone stack (**Figure 10**).

11 String 8A and pass through the middle A the thread originally exited from. Reinforce. Add an ear wire to the loop (**Figure 11**).

12 Make another top component following Steps 1–11.

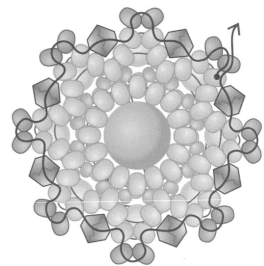

FIGURE 9

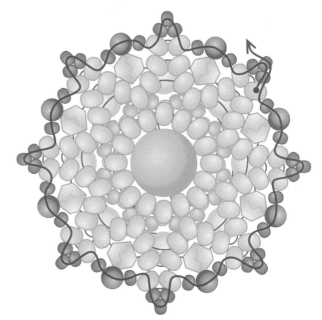

FIGURE 10

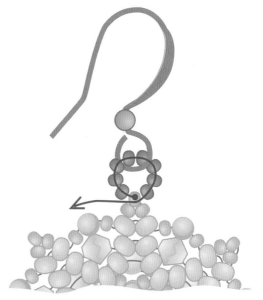

FIGURE 11

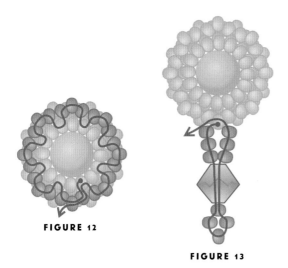

FIGURE 12

FIGURE 13

FRINGE COMPONENTS

13 With 36" (91.5 cm) of thread, repeat Steps 1–4 but use 1F instead of 1H and use A instead of B.

14 Weave down to the other row of A and come out of an A that doesn't match up with the 3A sets from the other side. This side of 3A should be offset from the first side. String 3A, skip over the next A, and pass through the next one. Repeat for a total of 8 sets of 3A. After adding the last set, step up into the first 2A of the first set added in this row (**Figure 12**).

15 String 3A, 1G, and 4A. Skip the last 3A and pass back through the first A strung and the G. String 3A and pass through the A the thread originally exited from (**Figure 13**).

16 Weave the thread so that it is coming out of the middle A of the set of 3A directly across from the little fringe added in Step 15. Cut a piece of chain that is 20 links long. Pass through the end link of the chain and then pass through the A the thread originally exited from. Reinforce one more time. Weave in and tie off the tail thread.

17 Repeat Steps 13–16 to make 5 more fringe components. However, add a 20-link piece of chain to one of them, add a 9-link piece of chain to 2 of them, and add a 3-link piece of chain to 2 more.

18 Weave the thread on a top component so that it is coming out of the middle A of the third set of 3A from Step 10. Pass through the end link of a chain with 20 links. Pass through the A the thread originally exited from. Reinforce one more time.

19 Add a chain piece with 9 links to the next set of 3A and a chain piece with 3 links to the next set of 3A. **Figure 14** illustrates how the chain pieces are attached.

20 Connect the other 3 chain pieces with the fringe components to the other top component following Step 18, but make sure they are in a mirror image.

FIGURE 14

glitz and glamour
NECKLACE

FINISHED SIZE

17" (43 cm)

SKILL LEVEL

Intermediate

MATERIALS

50 g gold electroplate size 15°
Japanese seed beads (A)

34 g crystal bronze-lined AB size
11° Japanese seed beads (B)

344 fuchsia 2mm
round crystals (C)

430 cream 3mm glass pearls (D)

7 fuchsia 13x6.5mm briolette
crystal drops

1 cream 6mm pearl

Size D nylon beading thread, gold

Thread conditioner

TOOLS

Size 12 beading needles

Scissors

**TECHNIQUES
YOU WILL USE**

FRINGE (PAGE 10)

PEYOTE (PAGE 11)

This piece looks much more complicated than it actually is. One basic component makes up the necklace—there are just a lot of them! You might not finish it in one evening, but I think it is well worth the time to make this luxurious necklace. I like to connect the components as I make them, but you can make all the components and then start connecting—either way works!

NECKLACE COMPONENT

1 With 36" (91.5 cm) of thread, string 4D. Pass through all 4 again and also pass through the first D again. Leave a 10" (25.5 cm) tail (**Figure 1, blue thread**).

2 String 5A and pass through the D the thread originally exited. String 1B and pass through the next D from Step 1. Repeat for a total of 4 sets. After adding the last set, step up into the first 3A of the first 5A added in this row (**Figure 1, red thread**).

3 String 1A, skip over the next A from Step 2, and pass through the next one. String 1B, skip over the next B from Step 2, and pass through the next A. String 1A, skip over the next A from Step 2, and pass through the next one. Repeat on each side. After adding the last A, step up into the first A added in this row (**Figure 2**).

4 String 1B and work a row of peyote by passing through the beads added in Step 3. There should be a total of 12B added in this row. After adding the last B, step up into the first B added in this row (**Figure 3**).

5 String 2A and pass through the next B from Step 4. Repeat for a total of 12 sets of 2A (**Figure 4**).

6 With the tail thread (it should be exiting from 1 of the D from Step 1), string 1D and pass through another D from Step 1 at an angle so that the D just added sits in the middle of the 4D from Step 1 (**Figure 5, blue thread**). Pass through the closest B from Step 2. String 2A, 1C, and 2A. Pass through the next B from Step 2. Repeat for a total of 4 sets (**Figure 5, red thread**). Weave in and tie off the tail thread.

7 Make 85 more components following Steps 1–6.

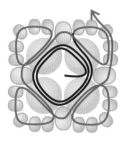
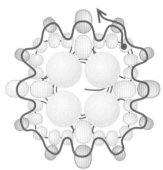

FIGURE 1

FIGURE 2

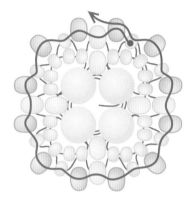

FIGURE 3

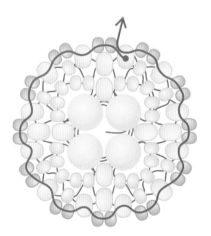

FIGURE 4

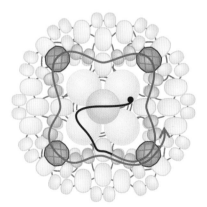

FIGURE 5

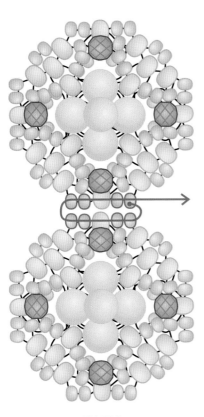

FIGURE 6

CONNECTING COMPONENTS

8 Weave a thread on a component so that it is coming out of a set of 2A from Step 5 that are on a corner (the corners are closest to the C that were added in Step 6). The thread should be exiting on the far side. Then pass through 2A, 1B, and 2A on the corner of another component. Pass through the previous 2A, 1B, and the 2A the thread originally exited from (**Figure 6**). Reinforce one more time.

9 To make the band part of the necklace, connect 2 components following Step 8. Then connect these in 3 places to another set of connected components. Stagger them slightly. **Figure 7** illustrates the 3 connections. The thread path is the same as it is in Step 8.

10 Connect 24 of the components together to make the first half of the band following Steps 8–9.

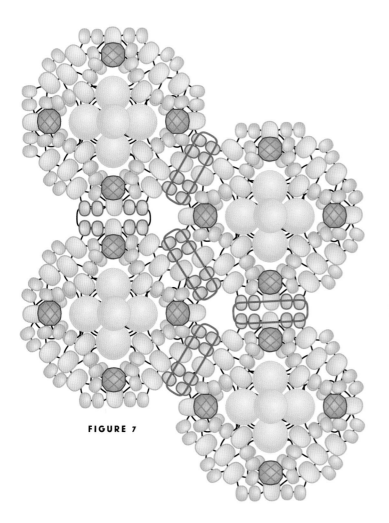

FIGURE 7

FIGURE 8

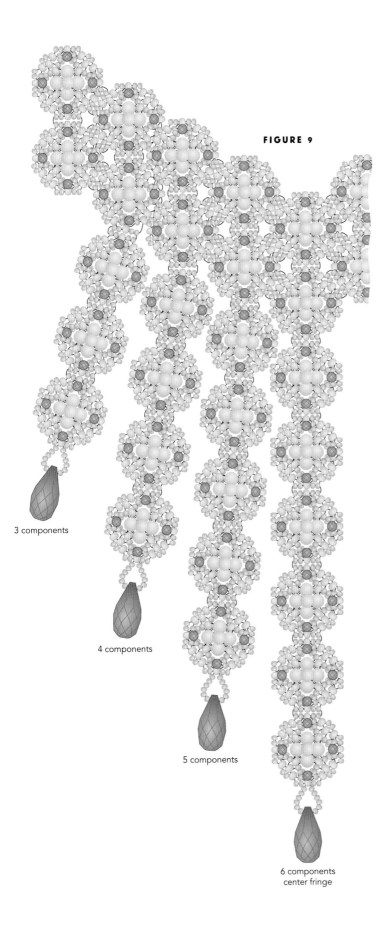

FIGURE 9

3 components

4 components

5 components

6 components
center fringe

11 Figure 8 illustrates the placement and connections for the center and second half of the band. There is a V pattern to the necklace, and the center set of components is the dip in the V. Connect 26 components to make the center and the second half of the band following Steps 8–9.

FRINGE

12 There are 7 fringe components connected to the band. The fringe components are only connected together on each side following Step 8. **Figure 9** illustrates the number of components in each fringe. Repeat the components on the other side of the center fringe in a mirror image to complete all 7 fringe components.

13 There is a drop bead attached to the last component of each fringe. The thread on the last component should be coming out of 1B directly across from the last connection. String 6A, 1 drop bead, and 6A. Pass through the B the thread originally exited from. Repeat on all 7 fringe components (**Figure 10**).

CLASP BEADS AND LOOPS

14 Weave a thread on the last component on the end at the top so that it is coming out of the fourth set of 2A, counting away from the connection of 2 components. String 3A, 1B, 1 6mm pearl, and 3A. Skip the last 3A and pass back through the 6mm pearl and the 1B. String 3A and pass through the 2A the thread originally exited from (**Figure 11**). Reinforce.

15 Weave a thread on the last top component on the other end so that it is coming out of the fourth set of 2A, counting away from the connection of a set of 2 components. String enough A to fit comfortably but snugly around the 6mm bead (**Figure 12**). Reinforce.

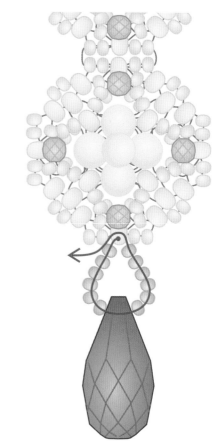

FIGURE 10

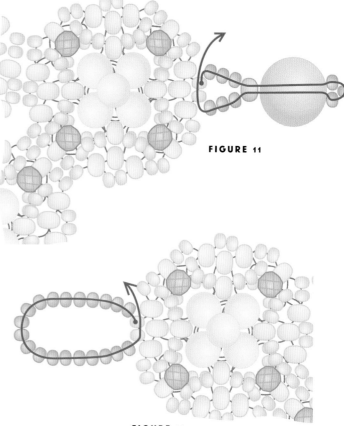

FIGURE 11

FIGURE 12

FINISHED SIZE

1½" (3.8 cm)

SKILL LEVEL

Intermediate

MATERIALS

3 g matte black size 15° Japanese seed beads (A)

3 g palladium electroplate size 15° Japanese seed beads (B)

4 g black size 11° cylinder beads (C)

3 g nickel silver electroplate size 11° Japanese seed beads (D)

16 jet 2mm round crystals (E)

16 fuchsia 3mm bicone crystals (F)

1 crystal 18mm crystal rivoli stone

Size D nylon beading thread, black

Thread conditioner

TOOLS

Size 12 beading needles

Scissors

TECHNIQUES YOU WILL USE

NETTING (PAGE 12)

PEYOTE (PAGE 11)

soiree
RING

I think big cocktail rings make a great fashion statement. They can be fun, elegant, and so very sparkly. I like to wear one or maybe two every chance I get. Since I live in a small rural town, that doesn't happen often, so I try to make up for it when I get to go to the big city. I used a large, sparkly rivoli for the center of this ring, and I think it is perfect for a night on the town!

RIVOLI BEZEL

1 With 90" (229 cm) of thread, string 32C and pass back through all 32C again. Also pass through the first C again (**Figure 1, green thread**). Leave a 6" (15 cm) tail.

2 Work a row of peyote with 16C, 1C in each stitch. After adding the last C, step up into the first C added in this row (**Figure 1, blue thread**).

3 Work another row of peyote with 16C, 1C in each stitch. After adding the last C, step up into the first C added in this row (**Figure 1, red thread**).

4 String 2A and pass through the next C from Step 3. Repeat for a total of 16 sets of 2A. After adding the last set, step up into the first 2A added in this row (**Figure 2**).

5 String 1D and pass through the next set of 2A from Step 4. Repeat for a total of 16D. After adding the last D, step up into the first D added in this row (**Figure 3, blue thread**).

6 String 3D and pass through the next D from Step 5. Repeat for a total of 16 sets of 3D. After adding the last set, step up into the next set of 2A from Step 4 (**Figure 3, red thread**).

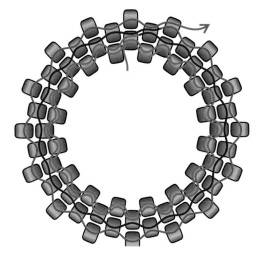

FIGURE 1

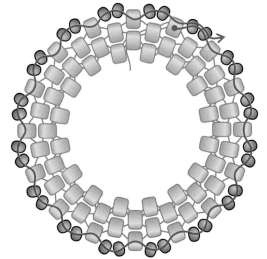

FIGURE 2

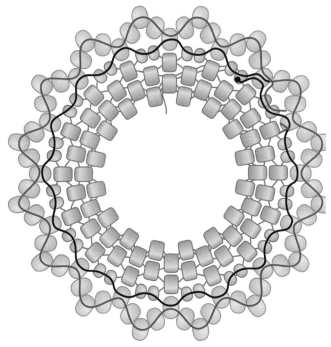

FIGURE 3

FIGURE 4

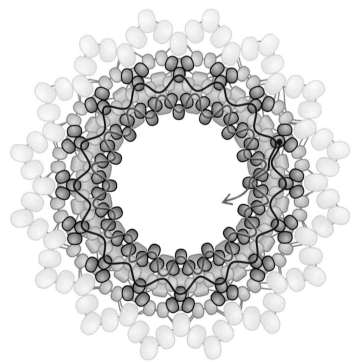

FIGURE 5

7 String 3A and pass through the next set of 2A from Step 4. This creates a point that sits on top of the previous beadwork. Repeat for a total of 16 sets of 3A. After adding the last set, step up into the first 2A of the first set of 3A added in this row (Figure 4).

8 String 3B and pass through the middle bead of the next set of 3A from Step 7. Repeat for a total of 16 sets of 3B. After adding the last set, step up into the first 2B of the first set of 3B added in this row (Figure 5, blue thread).

9 String 3A and pass through the middle bead of the next set of 3B from Step 8. Repeat for a total of 16 sets of 3A. After adding the last set, step up into the first 2A of the first set of 3A added in this row (Figure 5, red thread).

10 String 1D and pass through the middle bead of the next set of 3A from Step 9. Repeat for a total of 16D. Insert the rivoli into the beadwork, right side facing up (**Figure 6**). Reinforce this row one more time. Weave in and tie off the tail thread.

11 Weave the thread so that it is coming out of a middle bead of a set of 3D from Step 6. String 1B, 1F, and 1B. Pass through the next D from Step 6. Repeat for a total of 16 sets. After adding the last set, step up into the first set added in this row. This row will be a little ruffly (**Figure 7, blue thread**).

12 String 1E and pass through the next set of 1B, 1F, and 1B from Step 11. Repeat for a total of 16E. After adding the last E, step up into one of the F added in Step 11 (**Figure 7, red thread**).

13 String 1B and pass through the next E added in Step 12. String 1B and pass through the next F added in Step 11. Repeat for a total of 32B. After adding the last B, step up into the first B added in this row (**Figure 8, blue thread**).

FIGURE 6

FIGURE 7

FIGURE 8

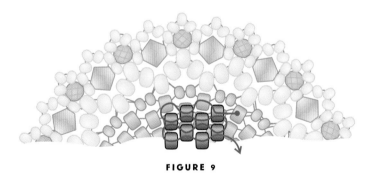

FIGURE 9

14 String 3B and pass through the next B added in Step 13. Repeat for a total of 32 sets of 3B (**Figure 8, red thread**).

RING BAND

15 Weave the thread to the back of the rivoli and come out of a C from Step 3. String 1C and pass through the next C from Step 3. Repeat one more time.

16 String 1C and pass back through the last C added in Step 15. String 1C and pass through the first C added in Step 15. This is the start of the ring band that will be a peyote strip 4C wide.

17 Continue working peyote until the strip is long enough to fit around your finger. Then attach the strip to the other side of the ring by zipping the C of the ring bezel and strip together (**Figure 9**). Reinforce.

all that glitters
LARIAT

FINISHED SIZE

33" (84 cm)

SKILL LEVEL

Advanced Beginner

MATERIALS

36 g permanent gold galvanized
size 15° Japanese seed beads (A)

6 g white opal gilt-lined size 15°
Japanese seed beads (B)

4 g 24k gold-lined size 11°
Japanese seed beads (C)

4 g gold electroplate size 11°
Japanese seed beads (D)

22 crystal AB 3mm
bicone crystals (E)

6 crystal AB 4mm
bicone crystals (F)

3 crystal AB 28x14mm
teardrop crystals

1 crystal AB 27mm round
crystal stone

Size D nylon beading thread, gold

Thread conditioner

TOOLS

Size 12 beading needles

Scissors

**TECHNIQUES
YOU WILL USE**

NETTING (PAGE 12)

This opulent lariat is made with gold and crystal AB, but it would also be striking in silver. You could make the strands longer or shorter to suit your personality. I love them long and swingy!

LARGE CRYSTAL BEZEL

1 With 72" (183 cm) of thread, string 12C and pass through all C again. Also pass through the first C again. Leave a 6" (15 cm) tail (**Figure 1, blue thread**).

2 String 9C and 3D. Pass back through the second D just added. String 1D and 9C. Pass through the C the thread originally exited from and also pass through the next 2C of the original circle from Step 1.

3 Repeat Step 2 for a total of 6 points. After adding the last point, weave the thread so that it is coming out of the sixth C of the first point (**Figure 1, red thread**).

4 String 3C and 3D. Pass back through the second D just added. String 1D and 3C. Pass through the last 6C of the next point and also pass through the C of the original circle from Step 1, and then pass up through the first 6C of the other side of the same point. Repeat for a total of 6 smaller points that sit between the large points (**Figure 2**).

5 Weave the thread so that it is coming out of a D at the tip of a point. String 3D and pass through the next D at the tip of the next point. Repeat for a total of 12 sets of 3D. Insert the 27mm crystal, right side facing up (**Figure 3**). Reinforce this row and pull snug.

FIGURE 1

FIGURE 2

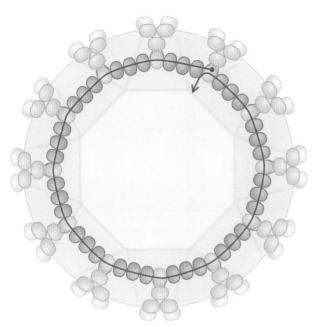

FIGURE 3

FIGURE 4

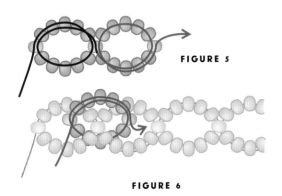

FIGURE 5

FIGURE 6

6 Weave the thread so that it is coming out of a first D on the right side of a point (the D next to the C of the point). The thread should be going toward the back of the crystal. String 1A, 1D, and 1A. Pass up through the next D on the left side of the next point. Pass down through the next D of the same point. Repeat, adding a total of 12 sets. After adding the last set, step up through the first 1A and 1D added in this row (**Figure 4, blue thread**). This row should sit right alongside the edge of the 27mm crystal.

7 String 1E and pass through the middle D of a set of 3D from Step 5 that is directly over the D the thread is exiting from. Pass back through the E. Pass through the D the thread originally exited from. Weave over to the next D of the next set from Step 6 and repeat. Repeat for a total of 12E (**Figure 4, red thread**). Weave in and tie off the tail thread.

DOUBLE CHAINS AND DROPS

8 With 72" (183 cm) of thread, string 1B, 5A, 1B, and 5A. Pass through the first B, the first 5A, and the second B (**Figure 5, blue thread**). Leave a 10" (25.5 cm) tail.

9 String 5A, 1B, and 5A. Pass through the B the thread is exiting from in the previous loop, the first 5A, and the 1B (**Figure 5, red thread**).

10 Repeat Step 9 until the chain is 28" (71 cm) long.

11 With 72" (183 cm) of thread, string 1B, 5A, 1B, and 5A. Pass through the opening (not a bead) of the first circle and the second circle of the first chain. Then pass through the first B, the next 5A, and the second B. Leave a 10" (25.5 cm) tail. This chain is made with the same thread path as the first chain, but it is interlocked with the first chain (kind of like those paper chains we made in kindergarten) (**Figure 6**).

12 Repeat Step 11 down the entire length of the first chain.

13 Make a second double chain 26" (66 cm) long following Steps 8–12.

14 Make a third double chain 24" (61 cm) long following Steps 8–12.

15 Weave a thread on the end of a double chain so that it is coming out of the B on the last link of the chain. String 6D, 1F, 3D, 1 drop bead, 3D, 1F, and 6D. Pass through the B the thread originally exited from (**Figure 7, blue thread**). String 6D, pass through the F, string 3D, pass through the drop bead, string 3D, pass through the F, string 6D, and pass through the B the thread originally exited from (**Figure 7, red thread**).

16 Repeat Step 15 on the other 2 chains.

17 On one end of the 28" (71 cm) chain, weave a thread so that it is coming out of the B on the end of the inside chain. String 5A and pass through a D added in Step 6 on the bezel. String 5A and pass through the B the thread originally exited from. Reinforce (**Figure 8**).

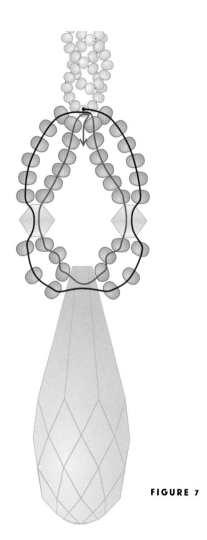

FIGURE 7

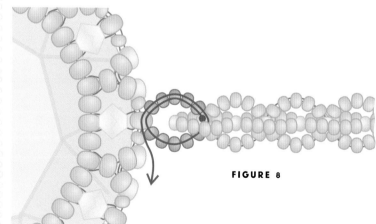

FIGURE 8

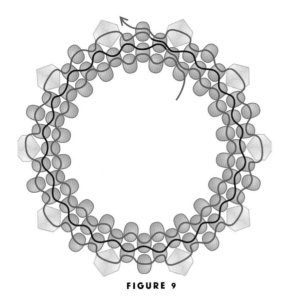

FIGURE 9

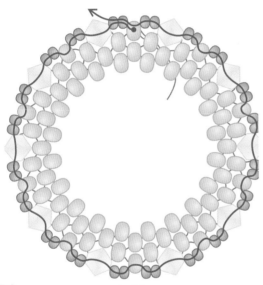

FIGURE 10

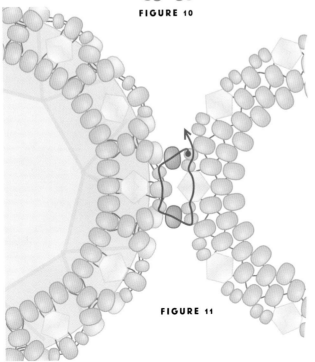

FIGURE 11

18 Repeat Step 17 with the 26" (66 cm) chain on the next D added in Step 6.

19 Repeat Step 17 with the 24" (61 cm) chain on the other side of the 28" (71 cm) chain at the D added in Step 6. This will stagger the length of the chains with the longest one in the middle.

OPEN RING

20 With 36" (91.5 cm) of thread, string 40D. Pass through all the beads again and also pass through the first D (**Figure 9, green thread**). Leave a 6" (15 cm) tail.

21 Work a row of peyote with 1D in each stitch. After adding the last D, step up into the first D added in this row (**Figure 9, blue thread**).

22 String 1D and pass through the next D from Step 21. String 1E and pass through the next D from Step 21. Repeat, adding a total of 10D and 10E. After adding the last E, step up into the first D added in this row (**Figure 9, red thread**).

23 String 2A and pass through the next E from Step 22. String 2A and pass through the next D from Step 22. Repeat, adding a total of 20 sets of 2A (**Figure 10**). Weave in and tie off the tail thread.

24 Weave the thread on the ring so that it is coming out of a set of 2A on the left side of an E added in Step 22. String 1D and pass through the set of 1A, 1D, and 1A added in Step 6 that is directly across from the connection of the middle chain. String 1D and pass through the 2A on the right side of the E (**Figure 11**). Reinforce.

madison avenue
BRACELET

FINISHED SIZE

8" (20.5 cm)

SKILL LEVEL

Intermediate

MATERIALS

6 g candlelight opal gilt-lined size 15° Japanese seed beads (A)

2 g gold bronze metallic size 15° Japanese seed beads (B)

6 g gold bronze metallic size 11° Japanese seed beads (C)

132 crystal dorado 2X 3mm bicone crystals (D)

2 crystal dorado 2X 4mm bicone crystals (E)

17 cream 8mm glass pearls (F)

Size D nylon beading thread, tan

Thread conditioner

TOOLS

Size 12 beading needles

Scissors

TECHNIQUES YOU WILL USE

CUBIC RIGHT-ANGLE WEAVE (PAGE 11)

PEYOTE (PAGE 11)

This design was inspired by a pearl bracelet an actress was wearing on a television show set in the 1960s. I love the retro feel, but I couldn't resist adding lots of crystals for a more modern look.

CRAW ENDS

1 With 72" (183 cm) of thread, string 4C. Pass through all the beads again and pass through the first C again (**Figure 1, blue thread**). Leave a 12" (30.5 cm) tail. This will be the base.

2 Work CRAW by stringing 3C; pass through the C the thread is exiting from and also pass through the next C in the base. This is the first wall (**Figure 1, red thread**).

3 String 2C and pass through the side C from Step 2 and also pass through the C of the base that the thread originally exited from and the first C added in this step. This is the second wall (**Figure 2**).

4 String 2C and pass through the next C of the base. Pass up through the C from Step 3 and also pass through the 2C just added, the next base bead, and up through the side C of the first wall. This is the third wall (**Figure 3**).

5 String 1C and pass down through the side bead of the third wall; pass through the base bead and pass up through the side bead of the first wall and the top 1C of the first wall. This is the fourth wall (**Figure 4**). Then pass through the top bead of each wall and also pass through the next top bead (**Figure 5**). Pull snug to firm up the cube shape (**Figure 6**). This completes 1 cube, and the top is now the base for the next cube.

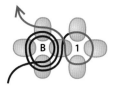

FIGURE 1

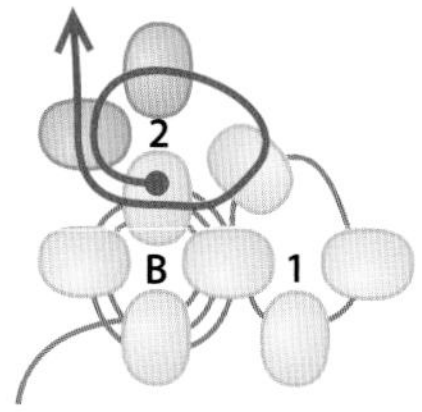

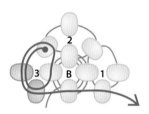

FIGURE 2

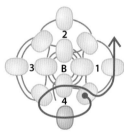

FIGURE 3

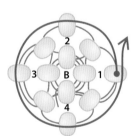

FIGURE 4

FIGURE 5

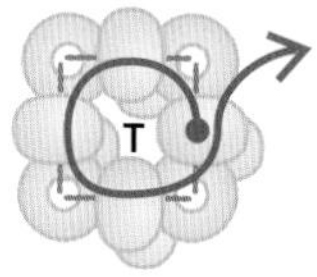

FIGURE 6

FIGURE 7

6 Keep working CRAW following Steps 2–5 until there are 8 cubes (**Figure 7**).

7 Work 3 more cubes off the end cube (**Figure 8**).

8 Work 7 cubes off the end cube of the 3 cubes added in Step 7 (**Figure 9**).

9 Work 1 cube off the end cube of the 7 cubes added in Step 8. Then connect the first cube and the cube just added to make a rectangle of the cubes with 8 cubes on the long sides and 4 cubes on the short sides (**Figure 10**).

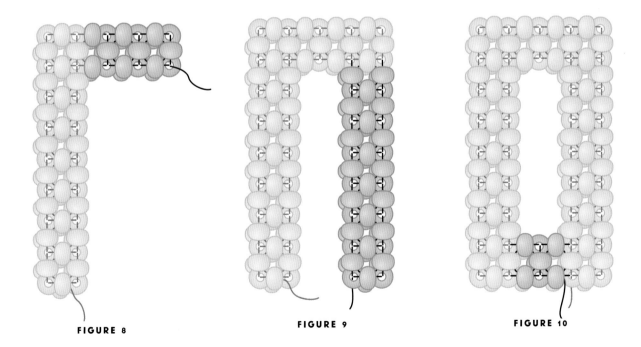

FIGURE 8

FIGURE 9

FIGURE 10

10 Weave the thread so that it is coming out of a C on the outside edge of a cube. String 1C and pass through the next C. Repeat all the way around the rectangle, adding a total of 24C. Weave over to the other side and repeat (**Figure 11**).

11 Weave the tail thread left earlier so that it is coming out of a side C on the top of a cube. String 1A and pass through the next C. If the thread is coming out of the top of the C, then pass through the bottom of the next C so that the A added sits in the middle of the cube. Repeat for a total of 20A (**Figure 12**). Weave in and tie off the tail and working threads.

12 Make a bar with 8 CRAW cubes with C for the other end of the bracelet, following Steps 1–6.

13 Weave the thread so that it is coming out of a C on the outside edge. String 1 C and pass through the next C. Repeat for a total of 18C. Weave over to the other side and repeat.

14 Add 8A down the middle of the bar, following Step 11 (**Figure 13**). Weave in and tie off the tail thread and the working thread.

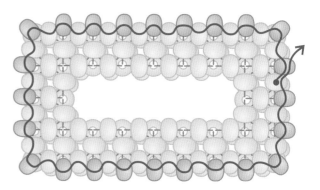

FIGURE 11

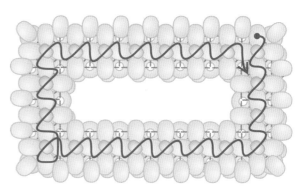

FIGURE 12

FIGURE 13

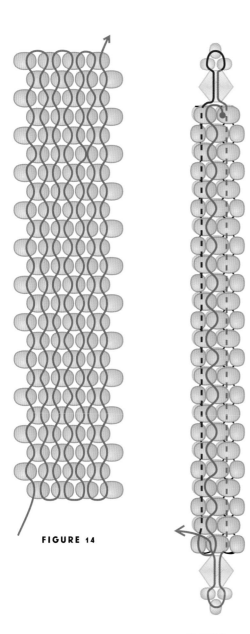

FIGURE 14

FIGURE 15

TOGGLE BAR

15 With 54" (137 cm) of thread, string 24C and work a piece of flat even-count peyote with C that has 4C on each end. Leave an 8" (20.5 cm) tail (Figure 14).

16 Fold the peyote piece in half and zip together the up beads on each side to form a tube. End with the thread coming out of the last C at the end of the tube. Pass down through the C with the tail thread coming out of it and come up the next C (Figure 15, green thread).

17 Pass the needle and thread through the center of the tube. String 1E and 3A (Figure 15, blue thread). Skip the last 3A and pass back through the E and the middle of the tube. String 1E and 3A. Skip the last 3A and pass back through the E and the middle of the tube (Figure 15, red thread). Reinforce several times.

18 Weave the thread so that it is coming out of the twelfth and thirteenth C, counting in from one end of the tube. String 8C and pass through the fifth C on the bottom edge of the CRAW bar that was added in Step 13. String 8C and pass through the twelfth and thirteenth C on the toggle bar. Reinforce (**Figure 16**). Weave in and tie off the tail and working threads.

CHAINS

19 Weave a new 72" (183 cm) length of thread so that it is coming out of the third C on a long side of the rectangle. String 5A, 1B, and 5A. Pass through the C the thread originally exited from and also go through the first 5A and 1B.

20 String 5A, 1B, and 5A. Pass through the B the thread originally exited from and also go through the first 5A and the 1B just added (**Figure 17**). Repeat for a total of 32 circles, counting the first circle made in Step 19.

21 String 5A and pass through the third C on a long side of the CRAW bar. Make sure the embellished side of the rectangle and bar are on the same side. String 5A and pass through the B the thread started in and also pass through the first 5A again and the third C on the bar.

22 String 1A, 1D, and 1A and pass through the next B. If the thread is exiting the C from the top, then go up the B from the bottom. If the thread is exiting from the bottom, pass through the B from the top. This will make the set of 1A, 1D, and 1A lie in the middle of the circle (**Figure 18**).

23 String 1A, 1D, and 1A and pass through the next B. Repeat until there are 33 sets, one in each circle. After adding the last set, pass through the third C the chain started in.

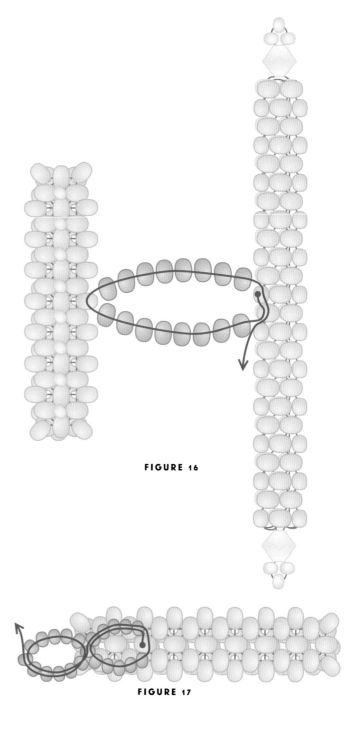

FIGURE 16

FIGURE 17

FIGURE 18

24 Repeat Steps 22–23 going down the chain again, adding the 1A, 1D, and 1A on the other side of the circles. Repeat for a total of 33 sets.

25 Repeat Steps 19–24 on the seventh C on the CRAW rectangle and bar.

26 Weave a new 36" (91.5 cm) length of thread so that it is coming out of the fifth C on the CRAW rectangle. String 1C and 1F until you have 17 sets. End with 1C. Pass through the fifth C on the CRAW bar. Pass back through all the Cs and Fs just added. Pass through the fifth C on the CRAW rectangle. Reinforce.

variation

I had a day-and-night theme in mind when I designed the Madison Avenue Bracelet. The variation shown here, with silver crystals and black pearls, is my night version.

diva
EARRINGS

I was playing around with brick stitch for a project, and I had the long oval crystals on my bead board with an idea to use them in a ring. But they found their way onto the brick-stitch piece I was working on instead. Thus the Diva Earrings were born. The metal bezel, which sits on the brick-stitch base, and the long lines of the crystals give the earrings their unique shape.

DIAMOND BASE

1 With 72" (183 cm) of thread, work a row of ladder stitch that is 3 stitches long, using 2B in each stitch (2-drop). Leave a 10" (25.5 cm) tail (**Figure 1**).

2 Work brick stitch using 2B in each stitch. String 4B, pass under the closest exposed thread loop, and go back through the fourth and third Bs strung. String 2B, pass under the next exposed thread loop, and pass back through the 2B strung (**Figure 2, blue thread**). String 2B, pass under the same thread loop, and pass back through the 2B strung to complete an increase (**Figure 2, red thread**).

3 Work 6 more rows, and increase each row by 1 stitch so that the eighth row has 10 stitches (**Figure 3**).

4 Work brick stitch using 2B in each stitch for 8 rows. Decrease by working only 1 stack of 2B in the last stitch of each row. The first decrease row will have 9 stitches. Continue to decrease each row by 1 stitch until you work down to 2 stitches in the eighth row (**Figure 4**).

FRINGE

5 The thread should be coming out of one of the 2B on the last row. String 6A, 1D, and 6A. Pass through the B next to the one that the thread originally exited from. This will make a little looped fringe. Weave up and come out of the last 2B on the row with 6 stitches (**Figure 5, green thread**).

BEZEL AND EMBELLISHMENT

6 String 2B, skip over the next row, and pass through the next 2B of the next row that are directly across from where the thread is exiting. Repeat three more times. There should be a total of 4 sets of 2B on top of the brick stitch diamond (**Figure 5, blue thread**).

FIGURE 1

FIGURE 2

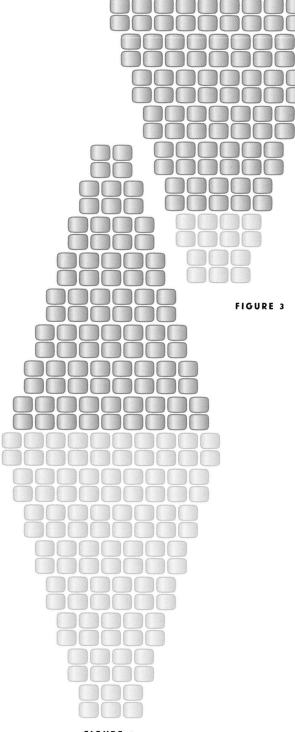

FIGURE 3

FIGURE 4

7 Weave over to the end set of 2B on the row with 6 stitches. Repeat Step 6 to add 4 more sets of 2B that are directly across from the 4 sets added in Step 6 (**Figure 5, red thread**).

8 Weave over and come out of the first set of 2B added in Step 6. String 3A and pass through the next set of 2B. Repeat two more times.

9 String 7A and pass through the next set of 2B on the other side of the diamond.

10 String 3A and pass through the next set of 2B. Repeat two more times.

11 String 7A and pass through the first set of 2B from Step 6 on the other side of the diamond. Also step up into the first 2A added in Step 8. Place the long oval crystal into the bezel, right side facing up (**Figure 6**).

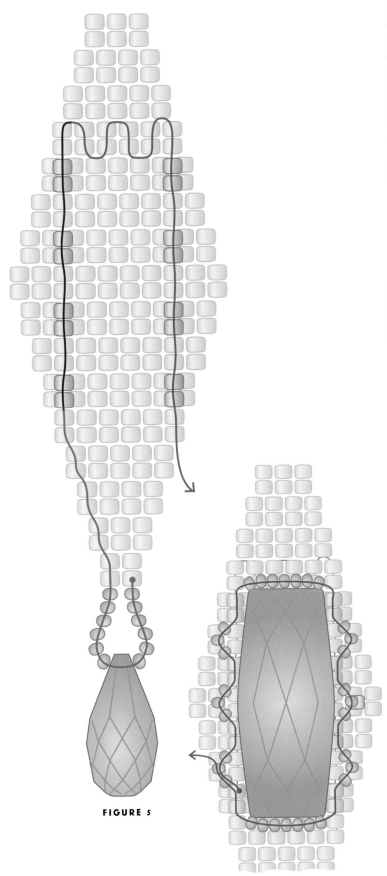

FIGURE 5

FIGURE 6

12 String 3A and pass through the middle bead of the next set of 3A. Repeat one more time. String 3A and pass through the last B of the set of 2B that is right before the 7A at the end. Also pass through the 7A at the end and come out of the first B of the next set of 2B.

13 String 3A and pass through the middle bead of the next set of 3A. Repeat two more times. String 3A and pass through the last B of the set of 2B that is right before the 7A at the end. Also pass through the 7A at the end and come out of the first B of the next set of 2B. String 3A and pass through the middle bead of the next set of 3A and also step up into the first 2A of the first 3A added in this round (Figure 7, blue thread).

14 String 1B and pass through the middle bead of the next set of 3A. Repeat one more time. String 3A and pass through the fourth A from the set of 7A at the end. String 3A and pass through the middle bead of the next set of 3A. String 1B and pass through the middle bead of the next set of 3A. Repeat two more times. Pull snug.

15 String 3A and pass through the fourth A from the set of 7A at the end. String 3A and pass through the middle bead of the next set of 3A. String 1B and pass through the middle bead of the next set of 3A (Figure 7, red thread). Pull snug.

16 Weave through the beads and come out of the last B of the last set of 2B added in Step 5. String 9A and pass through the first B of the next set of 2B. String 2A, 1C, and 2A. Pass through the 2B at the end of the row that has 10 stitches on the diamond. String 2A, 1C, and 2A. Pass through the last B of the last set of 2B.

17 String 9A and pass through the first B of the next set of 2B. String 2A, 1C, and 2A and pass through the 2B at the end the row with 10 stitches. String 2A, 1C, and 2A. Pass through the last B of the last set of 2B added in Step 5 (Figure 8).

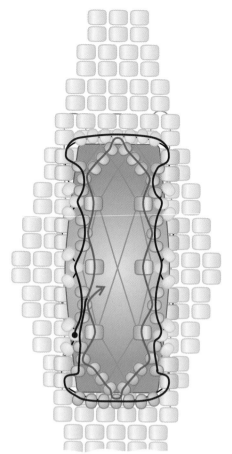

FIGURE 7

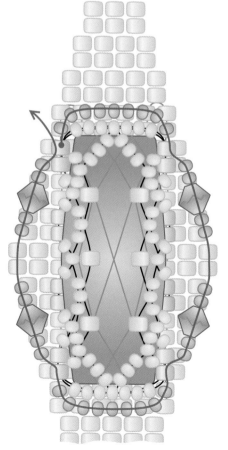

FIGURE 8

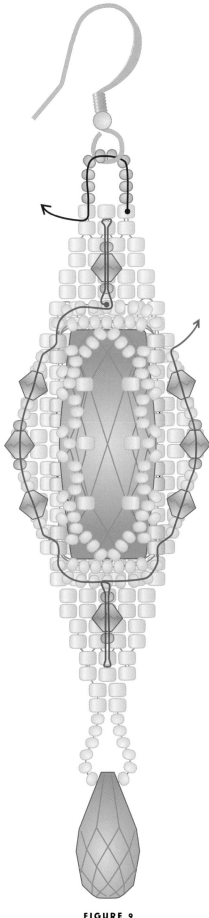

18 Weave the thread so that it is coming out of the fifth A of the set of 9A at the end of the crystal. String 1A, 1C, and 1A. Pass through the middle set of 2B on the last row on the diamond that has 3 stitches. Catch the thread at the end and pass back through the 2B and the 1A, 1C, and 1A and the fifth A of the set of 9A. Also pass through the next 4A of the 9A, the next B, and the next 2A, 1C, and 2A from Step 17.

19 String 1A, 1C, and 1A and pass through the next set of 2A, 1C, and 2A from Step 17. Also pass through the next B and the first 5A of the set of 9A at the end of the crystal. String 1A, 1C, and 1A. Pass through the 2B on the row with 3 stitches. Weave through the end beads and pass back through the 1A, 1C, and 1A and the fifth A of the set of 9A. Also pass through the next 4A, the next B, and the next 2A, 1C, and 2A.

20 String 1A, 1C, and 1A. Pass through the next 2A, 1C, and 2A. Weave in the thread and tie it off (**Figure 9, red thread**).

21 The tail thread should be coming out of the end stitch on the last row with 3 stitches. String 10A and pass through the third set of 2B and the loop of an ear wire (**Figure 9, blue thread**). Reinforce.

22 Repeat Steps 1–21 to make the second earring.

FIGURE 9

FINISHED SIZE

8½" (21.5 cm)

SKILL LEVEL

Intermediate

MATERIALS

7 g silver brass metallic iris size 15° Japanese seed beads (A)

7 g silver brass metallic iris size 11° Japanese seed beads (B)

5 g silver-lined teal size 11° Japanese seed beads (C)

168 teal 2mm glass pearls (D)

56 blue zircon 3mm bicone crystals (E)

7 light turquoise 14x10mm oval crystal stones (F)

1 aqua 8mm fire-polished crystal (G)

Size D nylon beading thread, turquoise

Thread conditioner

TOOLS

Size 12 beading needles

Scissors

TECHNIQUES YOU WILL USE

NETTING (PAGE 12)

PEYOTE (PAGE 11)

marquise
BRACELET

This bracelet features oval crystals for which I created a bezel that has a high profile with a marquise shape. I really like working with crystal stones; those of you familiar with my work may have noticed that. There are so many beautiful ways to create bezels for them.

BEZELS

1 With 72" (183 cm) of thread, string 24A; pass through all 24A again and also pass through the first A again. Leave an 8" (20.5 cm) tail (Figure 1, green thread).

2 Work a row of peyote with 12A (1A in each stitch). Step up into the first A added in this row (Figure 1, blue thread).

3 Work a row of peyote with 12C (1C in each stitch). Step up into the first C added in this row (Figure 1, red thread).

4 Work a row of peyote with 12B (1B in each stitch). Step up into the first B added in this row (Figure 2, blue thread).

5 String 3A and pass through the next B added in Step 4. Repeat a total of twelve times. Step up into the first 2A added in this row (Figure 2, red thread).

6 String 1A, 1C, and 1A. Pass through the middle bead of the next 3A added in Step 5. Repeat a total of twelve times. Step up into the first A and C added in this row (Figure 3).

7 String 1B and pass through the next C added in Step 6. Repeat a total of twelve times. Pull snug. This row will start to cup up. Step up into the first B added in this row (Figure 4).

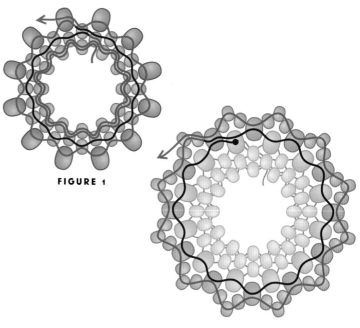

FIGURE 1

FIGURE 2

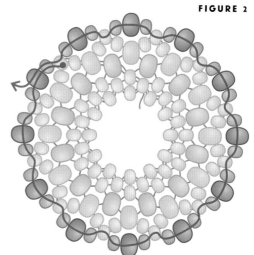

FIGURE 3

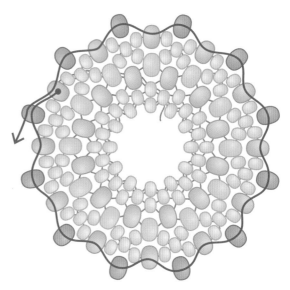

FIGURE 4

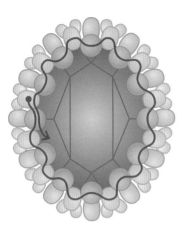

FIGURE 5

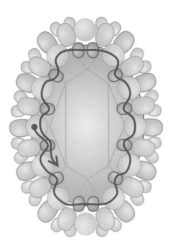

FIGURE 6

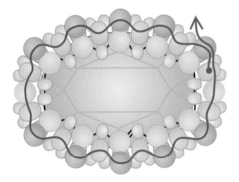

FIGURE 7

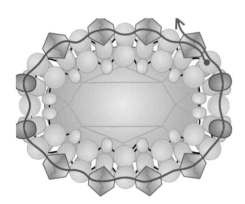

FIGURE 8

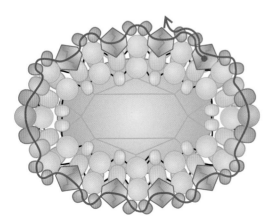

FIGURE 9

8 Work a row of peyote with 12D (1D in each stitch). Step up into the first D added in this row. Insert 1F (right side facing up) and pull snug (**Figure 5**). The crystal stone will be very loose in the bezel at this point.

9 Pinch the bezel on the long sides so that 1D pops out on the short ends. Work a row of peyote with 1A in each step except at the ends where the 1D is sticking out. At the ends, string 2A and skip over the 1D that sticks out. Pull snug. For this row, there should be 4A on each long side and 2A at each end (**Figure 6**).

10 Weave the thread so that it is coming out of the B added in Step 7 that is on the right side of the 1D at a short end. String 1D and pass through the next B from Step 7. Repeat a total of five times. Weave through the beads at the end and repeat on the other long side. There should be a total of 10D added in this row. Step up into the first D added in this row (**Figure 7**).

11 String 1E and pass through the next D from Step 10. Repeat three more times. String 1C and pass through the D at the short end from Step 8 that was previously skipped over. String 1C and pass through the next D from Step 10. Then add 4E on the other long side and 2C at the other short end (**Figure 8**). There should be 4E on each long side and 2C at each short end in this row.

12 Add 5 sets of 2A on the long sides (between the Es) and add 1B, 1D, and 1B at the short ends between the 2C from Step 11 (**Figure 9**).

13 Make 6 more components following Steps 1–12.

CONNECTIONS

14 Weave a thread on a component so that it is coming out of the D at one of the short ends of the bezel. String 1B and pass through the 1D at the short end of another component. String 1B and pass through the D the thread originally exited from (**Figure 10**). Reinforce one more time.

15 String 1B and pass through the 1C directly below the 1D. String 1B and pass through the 1D the thread originally exited from. Also pass through the first B added and the 1C and the 1B of the component directly below the 1C (**Figure 11**).

16 String 5B and pass through the corresponding 1B on the other component. String 5B and pass through the 1B the thread originally exited from (**Figure 12**). Reinforce one more time.

17 Pass through the 1C on the second component above the 1B. String 1B and pass through the 1D. String 1B and pass through the 1C the thread originally exited. Weave in and tie off the thread.

18 Connect the remaining components following Steps 14–17.

CLASP BEAD AND LOOP

19 Weave a thread on an end component so that it is coming out of the 1C at the short end directly below the 1D at the tip. String 3B, 1C, 1G, and 3B. Skip the last 3B and pass back through the 1G and 1C. String 3B and pass through the 1C the thread originally exited from (**Figure 13**). Reinforce.

20 Weave a thread on the other end component so that it is coming out of the 1C at the short end. String enough B to fit comfortably but snugly around the 1G (**Figure 14**). Reinforce.

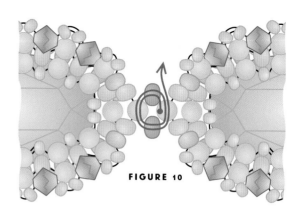

FIGURE 10

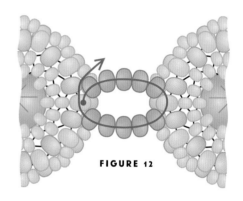

FIGURE 11

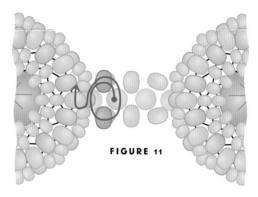

FIGURE 12

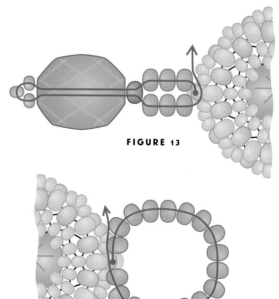

FIGURE 13

FIGURE 14

FINISHED SIZE

7" (18 cm)

SKILL LEVEL

Advanced Beginner

MATERIALS

2 g 24k gold-lined size 15°
Japanese seed beads (A)

12 g bronze metallic iris size
11° cylinder seed beads (B)

98 fuchsia 3mm
bicone crystals (C)

34 amethyst 4mm
bicone crystals (D)

Size D nylon beading thread, gold

Thread conditioner

TOOLS

Size 12 beading needles

Scissors

**TECHNIQUES
YOU WILL USE**

BRICK (PAGE 12)

PEYOTE (PAGE 11)

This light and airy bracelet is made primarily with brick stitch, which I think is a great, underappreciated stitch. Brick stitch is a sturdy stitch and is easily embellished. In this case, I embellished it with lots of crystals for maximum bling.

BRICK STITCH STRIPS

1 With 72" (183 cm) of thread, string 2B. Pass through both B again and manipulate the beads so that they sit side by side. Leave a 10" (25.5 cm) tail.

2 Work a row of brick stitch with 3B.

3 Work a row of brick stitch with 4B.

4 Work a row of brick stitch with 5B.

5 Work a row of brick stitch with 6B.

6 Repeat Steps 4–5 two more times (Figure 1).

7 Work a row of brick stitch with 5B.

8 Work a row of brick stitch with 4B.

9 Work a row of brick stitch with 3B.

10 Work a row of brick stitch with 2B.

11 Work a row of brick stitch with 3B.

12 Work a row of brick stitch with 2B (Figure 2).

13 Repeat Steps 2–12 seven more times, then repeat Steps 2–10 for a total of 9 units on the strip. On the last unit, end with a row of 2B.

14 Repeat Steps 1–13 for a second strip. Set the 2 strips aside for now.

15 Make 1 more strip following Steps 1–13. However, on this strip do add the last 2 rows on the ninth unit (Steps 11 and 12).

16 Work a row of brick stitch with 3B.

17 Work a row of brick stitch with 4B.

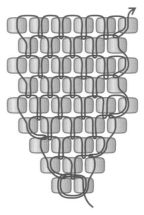

FIGURE 1

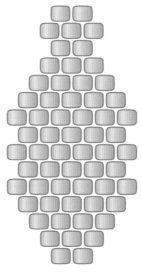

FIGURE 2

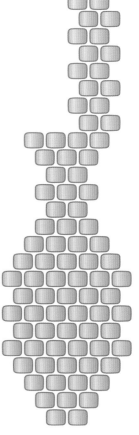

FIGURE 3

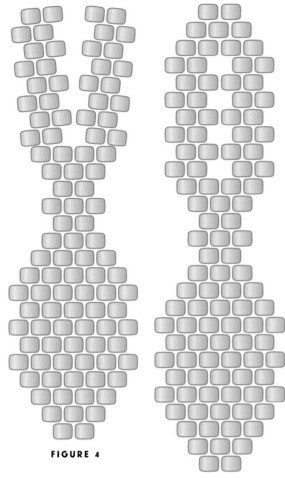

FIGURE 4

FIGURE 5

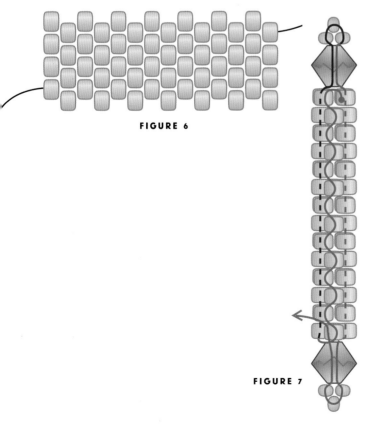

FIGURE 6

FIGURE 7

18 Work 8 rows of brick stitch with 2B in each row off of the first stitch on the last row of 4B (Figure 3).

19 Weave through the beads and come out of the other end bead on the row of 4B from Step 17. Work 8 rows of brick stitch with 2B in each row off the first stitch on this end (Figure 4).

20 Pass down through the second B of the last set of 2B and pass up through the next B on the next set of 2B. Pass down through the second B of the first set again and pass back up through the first bead of the second set. This will pull the 2 sets of 2B together and make a row of 4B. Then weave through the beads and come out of an end B.

21 Work a row of brick stitch with 3B.

22 Work a row of brick stitch with 2B (Figure 5). This completes the third strip and the tenth unit with the opening for the toggle bar. This will be the center strip of the bracelet.

TOGGLE BAR

23 With 36" (91.5 cm) of thread, string 14B. Then work flat even-count peyote until there are 4B on each end (Figure 6).

24 Fold the beadwork and pass through the up beads on both sides to zip the beads together to form a tube. At the end, pass down through the B that has the tail thread exiting it (Figure 7, green thread). Pass up through the next B. Pass the thread through the center of the tube. String 1D and 3A; skip the 3A and pass back through the 1D and the center of the tube. String 1D and 3A (Figure 7, blue thread); skip the 3A and pass back through the center of the tube (Figure 7, red thread). Reinforce and tie off the tail thread.

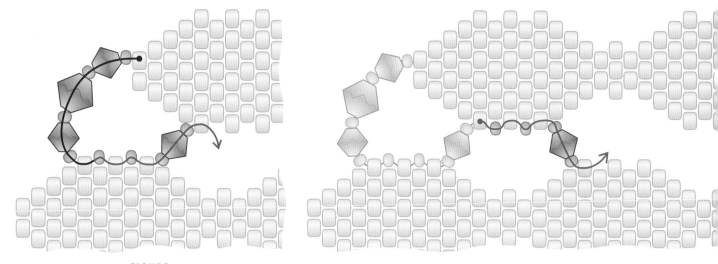

FIGURE 8

FIGURE 9

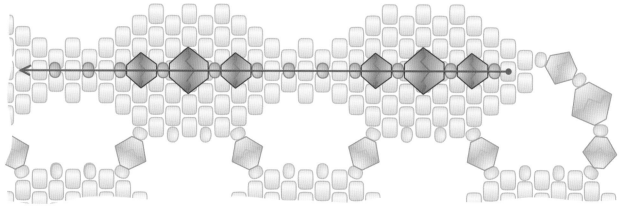

FIGURE 10

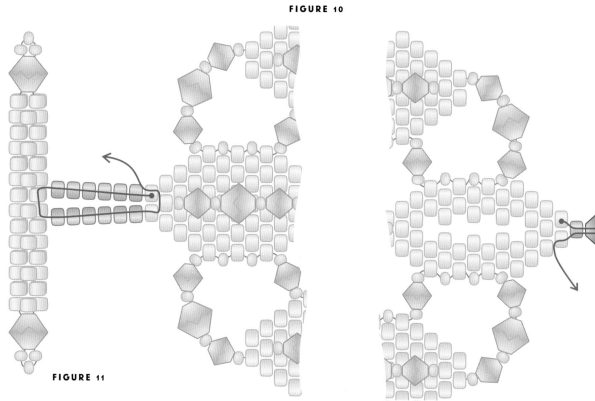

FIGURE 11

FIGURE 12

CONNECTIONS

25 Weave a thread on a side strip (one without the toggle opening) so that it is coming out of a B on the end row with 2B. Position the strip so that the B the thread is exiting from is on the outside. String 1A, 1C, 1A, 1D, 1A, 1C, and 1A and pass through the end B on the row with 6B on the center strip end unit (**Figure 8, blue thread**).

26 String 1A and pass through the next B that sticks out. Repeat one more time. String 1A, 1C, and 1A and pass through the B of the side strip on the row with 6B (**Figure 8, red thread**). String 1A and pass through the next B that sticks out. Repeat one more time. String 1A, 1C, and 1A and pass through the B of the next unit on the center strip that has 6B (**Figure 9**).

27 Repeat Step 26 until all the units are connected on the side and center strips. After adding the last 2A on the center strip, repeat Step 25 to add the end beads.

28 Weave the thread so that it is coming out of the middle B on the row of 3B on the end unit of the side strip. String 1A, 1C, 1A, 1D, 1A, 1C, and 1A and pass through the middle bead of the next row of 3B on the same unit. String 1A and pass through the middle bead of the next row of 3B (it will be the row between the units). String 1A and pass through the middle B of the next row of 3B on the next unit (**Figure 10**). Repeat until all the units on the side strip are embellished.

29 Repeat Steps 25–28 with the other side strip.

30 Weave a thread on the center strip on the end without the toggle opening so that it is coming out of the end row with 2B. String 6B and pass through the seventh and eighth Bs on the toggle bar. String 6B and pass through the B next to the one the thread originally exited from (**Figure 11**). Reinforce.

31 Repeat Step 28 on the center strip to embellish the top. Do not embellish the unit with the toggle opening.

32 Weave the thread so that it is coming out of one of the 2B at the end of the open unit. String 1B, 1D, and 1A. Skip the 1A and pass back through the D and the B. Pass through the B on the end row that is next to the one that the thread originally exited from (**Figure 12**). Reinforce and tie off the tail thread.

mixed-metals
CUFF

FINISHED SIZE

7½" (19 cm)

SKILL LEVEL

Advanced Beginner

MATERIALS

4 g gold electroplate size 15°
Japanese seed beads (A)

9 g palladium electroplate size
11° cylinder seed beads (B)

23" (58.5 cm) gold/blue zircon
24pp (3mm) cup chain

1 silver 20mm slide clasp with bar

Size D nylon beading thread, gray

Smoke 6 lb FireLine

Thread conditioner

TOOLS

Size 12 beading needles

Scissors

**TECHNIQUES
YOU WILL USE**

BRICK (PAGE 12)

PEYOTE (PAGE 11)

I had been collecting cup chain, but I had not used it in a project until this one. It was the perfect fit with the metal clasp because my idea for this design was to mix gold and silver. The blue zircon crystals of the cup chain add a punch of color that complements the silver and gold. Other jewel tones, such as amethyst and fuchsia, would also look great in this design.

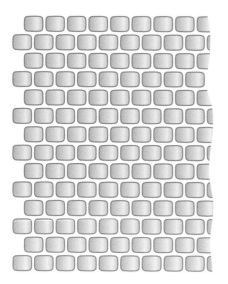

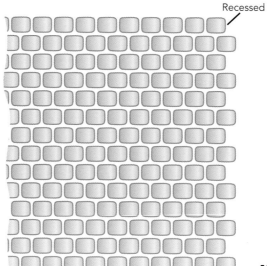

Recessed

FIGURE 1

FIGURE 2

FIGURE 3

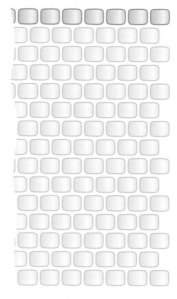

FIGURE 4

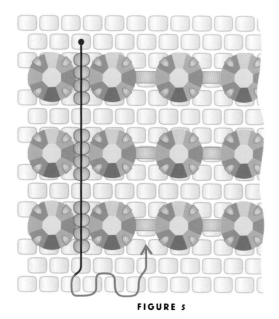

FIGURE 5

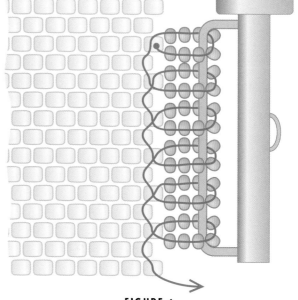

FIGURE 6

BAND

1 With 72" (183 cm) of thread, string 14B. Leave a 12" (30.5 cm) tail. Work flat even-count peyote with B to make a band that is 6½" (16.5 cm) long. End the band with a row so that one long side has beads sticking out at both ends, and the other long side has a recessed bead on both ends (**Figure 1**).

2 Now a brick-stitch row is going to be added to the long side with the recessed beads at the ends.

This will make a total of 15 rows. The thread should be coming out of the end bead on the last row on the recessed side. String 2B; pass under the first thread between the beads of the peyote and pass up through the second B (**Figure 2**).

3 String 1B; pass under the next thread between the beads of the peyote and pass back up through the B just added (**Figure 3**). Keep repeating to the end of the band. To add the last B, go under the last thread again. The B added in the brick-stitch row should stick out on both ends like the other long end of the peyote band (**Figure 4**).

CUP-CHAIN EMBELLISHMENT

4 Cut the cup chain into three 7½" (19 cm) pieces. This will be a little more than is needed, but it is better to have a few extra cups than not enough. Also, it is best to use FireLine to attach the cup chain to the band, as it will not fray if it catches on the cup chain like the nylon thread will.

5 Weave 72" (183 cm) of FireLine on the band so that it is coming out of the third B of the second row of the band. String 4A, skip over 3 rows, and pass through the next B directly across from the one the thread originally exited from. Before the stitch is pulled tight, put the first cup of a piece of chain under the 4A so that the 4A sit on top of the metal between the cups. Pull the stitch snug.

6 String 4A, skip over 3 rows, and pass through the next B directly across from the one the thread originally exited from. Put the second piece of cup chain under the stitch and pull snug.

7 Repeat Step 6 with the third piece of chain (**Figure 5, blue thread**).

8 Pass through the next B of the next row of peyote so that the thread is coming out of the last bead on the side of the band. Pass down through the next B and come up through the next B on the last row. Then pass down through the next 2B (**Figure 5, red thread**).

9 String 4A; pass between the next cups, skip over 3 rows, and pass through the next B in line with the one the thread originally exited from. Repeat two more times.

10 Keep repeating Steps 8–9 to attach the 3 pieces of cup chain to the band. Watch the spacing as you work; sometimes you will need to adjust the spacing a little. There should be 1B or 2B skipped between the 4A connections that attach the cup chain to the band. The 3 connections of 4A should fit comfortably over the space between the cups. What will always remain the same is that you start in the second row, skip over 3B, and pass through the next row to attach the 4A to the band. This will keep the cup chain lined up evenly as you work down the band. The band will start to curve somewhat as you attach the cup chain.

11 After attaching the cup chain all the way down the band, cut off any excess cups. They should end as close to the end of the band as possible.

12 Weave a thread so that it is coming out of the second up bead at the short end of the band going toward the beadwork. String 8A, pass through the bar of the clasp, and pass through the same B the thread originally exited from. Also pass through the next 2B so that the thread is coming out of the next up bead. Repeat five more times (**Figure 6**).

13 Repeat Step 12 with the second half of the clasp on the other end.

FINISHED SIZE

17" (43 cm)

SKILL LEVEL

Intermediate

MATERIALS

6 g bronze metallic iris size 15°
Japanese seed beads (A)

14 g bronze metallic iris size 11°
Japanese seed beads (B)

4 g silver-lined dark fuchsia size
11° Japanese seed beads (C)

114 eggplant 2mm
glass pearls (D)

24 fuchsia 4mm
bicone crystals (E)

4 volcano 12mm crystal
rivoli stones (F)

3 crystal lilac shadow 30x20mm
faceted pear crystal stones

1 fuchsia 8mm round crystal

Size D nylon beading thread,
burgundy

3 pieces 3" x 2" (7.5 x 5 cm)
backing (heavyweight interfacing
or Lacy's Stiff Stuff)

3 pieces 2" x 2" (5 x 5 cm)
Ultrasuede, burgundy

Toothpicks

Thread conditioner

E-6000 adhesive

TOOLS

Size 12 beading needles

Scissors

TECHNIQUES
YOU WILL USE

BACKSTITCH FOR BEAD
EMBROIDERY (PAGE 13)

EDGING FOR BEAD
EMBROIDERY (PAGE 13)

NETTING (PAGE 12)

PEYOTE (PAGE 11)

lotus
NECKLACE

This project is a mix of beadweaving and bead embroidery. The shape of the crystals reminded me of the petals of a lotus flower. Those beautiful crystals and the large pear crystals make this a statement piece fit for a special night out.

BACKSTITCH AND CRYSTAL PEAR BEZEL

1 Use a toothpick to spread a thin layer of E-6000 adhesive to the back side of a pear crystal. Set the crystal in the center of one backing piece and press firmly into place. You can push the backing up around the crystal and hold in place for a little while to help the edges of the crystal to adhere to the backing. You can always go back and use the toothpick to put a dab more glue on the areas that do not stick the first time. Try not to get any glue on the backing outside of the crystal, as it will be hard to sew through when it dries.

2 Put a knot in a 72" (183 cm) piece of thread. Come up from the back alongside the edge of the crystal. String 2B and pass down through the backing at the end of the 2B. Come back up through the backing at the front of the 2B and pass through them again (**Figure 1, green thread**). String 2B and pass down through the backing at the end of the 2B. Come back up through the backing between the first and second beads and pass through the next 3B (**Figure 1, blue thread**). Keep adding 2B and coming back up and passing through 3B (**Figure 1, red thread**). This connects the previous group of 2B with the new group of 2B. Work all the way around the crystal. This backstitch row needs to be an even number of beads.

3 String 1B, skip over the next B of the backstitch row, and pass through the next B. Continue working peyote stitch with 1B in each stitch until you have gone all the way around the crystal. Step up into the first B added in this row (**Figure 2, blue thread**).

4 Work 1 more row of peyote stitch with 1A in each stitch (**Figure 2, red thread**).

5 Weave through the beads of the bezel and go down through the backing. Then come back up through the backing close to the bezel and work another row of backstitch following Step 2. This row does not have to be an even number (**Figure 3**).

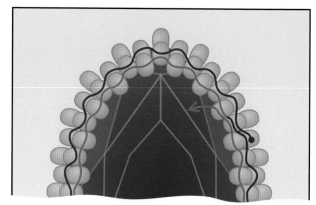

FIGURE 1

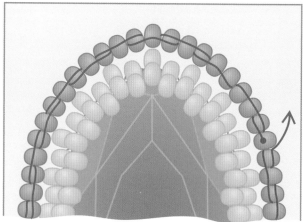

FIGURE 2

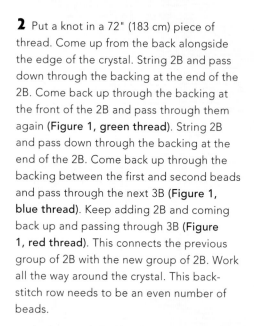

FIGURE 3

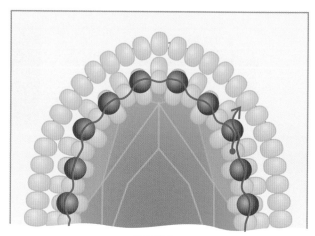

FIGURE 4

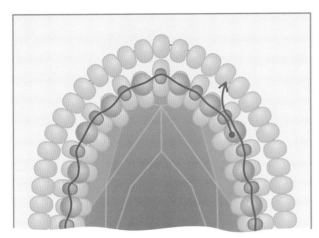

FIGURE 5

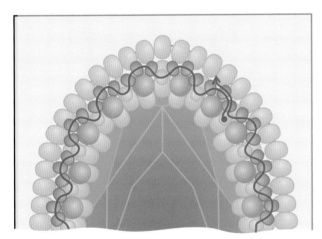

FIGURE 6

FIGURE 7

6 Then weave back up and come out of a B from Step 3. String 1D and pass through the next B from Step 3. The D added should stick out on the side of the bezel. Continue adding D until you have gone all the way around the crystal. Step up into the first D added in this row (**Figure 4**).

7 String 1A and pass through the next D from Step 6. Repeat all the way around the crystal. Step up into the first A added in this row (**Figure 5**).

8 String 3A and pass through the next A from Step 7. Repeat all the way around the crystal (**Figure 6**). Weave the thread down through the bezel and tie it off behind the backing.

9 Trim the backing close to the beadwork, making sure not to cut any threads. Make it as neat as possible. Spread a thin layer of E-6000 adhesive on the back of the bead-work with a toothpick. Then place the crystal onto a piece of Ultrasuede. Press down firmly into place. Let the glue dry. Then trim the Ultrasuede to match the backing.

EDGING

10 Anchor 54" (137 cm) of thread in the beadwork and come out at the edge of the Ultrasuede. String 2B; catch the suede about a bead's width over from where the thread originally exited and pass back up through the second B (**Figure 7, green thread**).

11 String 1B; catch the suede about a bead's width over from where the thread originally exited and pass back up through the B just added. Continue all the way around the crystal (**Figure 7, blue thread**). After adding the last B, pass down through the first B added in this row, catch the suede, and pass back up through it. This connects the edging at the first and last bead (**Figure 7, red thread**). Make 2 more crystal pear bezels.

NETTED BEZEL

12 String 12A and pass through all 12A again; also pass through the first A again to make a small circle. Leave a 6" (15 cm) tail (**Figure 8, green thread**).

13 Work a row of peyote stitch with 1B in each stitch. Step up into the first B added in this row (**Figure 8, blue thread**).

14 String 1A, 1B, and 1A and pass through the next B from Step 13. Repeat five more times. Step up into the first 1A and 1B added in this row (**Figure 8, red thread**).

15 String 2A, 1B, and 2A and pass through the next 1B added in Step 14. Repeat five more times. Step into the first 2A and 1B added in this row (**Figure 9, blue thread**).

16 Repeat Step 15. Pull snug so that the bezel starts to cup up (**Figure 9, red thread**).

17 Insert 1F into the beadwork, right side facing up. Repeat Step 15. Pull snug.

18 String 3A and pass through the next B from Step 17. Repeat five more times (**Figure 10**). Reinforce this row.

19 Weave the thread so that it is coming out of a B from Step 17. String 1A, 1D, and 1A and pass through the next B from Step 17. Repeat five more times.

20 Weave the thread so that it is coming out of a B from Step 16. String 1A, 1E, and 1A and pass through the next B from Step 16. Repeat five more times (**Figure 11**). Tie off the tail thread. Make 3 more netted bezels.

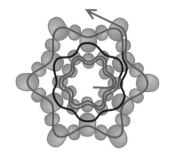

FIGURE 8

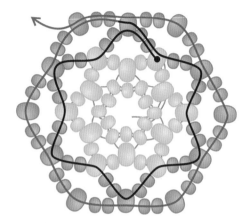

FIGURE 9

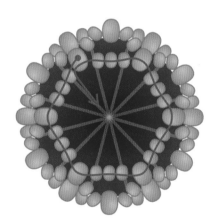

FIGURE 10

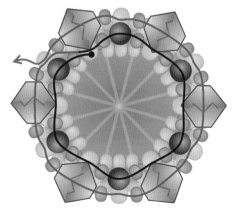

FIGURE 11

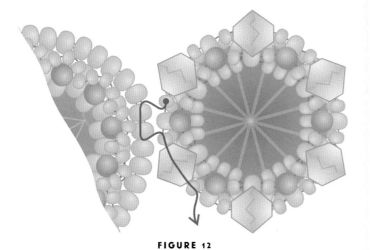

FIGURE 12

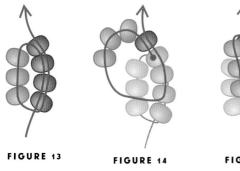

FIGURE 13   **FIGURE 14**   **FIGURE 15**

CONNECTIONS

21 The netted bezels are connected to the pear crystals on the sides near the top. There is not a set bead to go through; the connections are centered visually (in other words, eyeball it). Weave a thread on a netted bezel so that it is coming out of an A after an E added in Step 20. Then pass through 2B on the backstitch row from Step 5 on a crystal pear bezel on the top side. Pass through the next A in front of the next E from Step 20 (**Figure 12**).

22 Connect the remaining crystal pear bezels and the netted bezels following Step 21. Alternate between a netted bezel and a pear bezel. The netted bezels are connected to the pear bezels directly across from the first connection so that there is 1E between the connections. Make the placement of the connections so that the bezels have a slight curve to them. Reinforce the connections after you make sure the placement looks right.

SPIRAL ROPE

23 With 72" (183 cm) of thread, string 4C and 3B and pass through the 4C again (**Figure 13**). Leave a 12" (30.5 cm) tail.

24 String 1C and 3B. Pass through the last 3C of the previous 4 and also pass through the 1C just added (**Figure 14**). Move the 3B over so that they sit right next to the previous 3B and pull the thread snug (**Figure 15**).

25 Repeat Step 24 until the rope is 5" (12.5 cm) long. Put a needle on the tail thread. It should be coming out of one of the 2 beads at the end of the rope. Pass through the 1A, 1B, and 1A between the 2E directly across from the netted bezel connected to an end pear crystal. Pass through the other bead on the end of the rope (**Figure 16**). Reinforce.

26 Repeat Steps 23–25 on the other netted bezel on the other side of the beadwork.

CLASP BEAD AND LOOP

27 The thread should be coming out of the C at the end of one of the ropes. String 3B, 1C, the 8mm bead, and 3B. Skip the 3B and pass back through the 8mm bead and the 1C. String 3B and pass through the C the thread originally exited from (**Figure 17**). Reinforce.

28 The thread on the other rope should be coming out of the end C. String enough B to fit comfortably but snugly around the 8mm bead. Pass through the C the thread originally exited from (**Figure 18**). Reinforce.

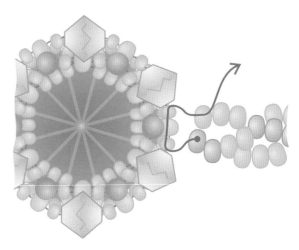

FIGURE 16

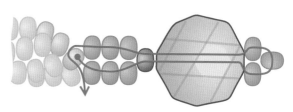

FIGURE 17

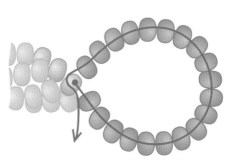

FIGURE 18

FINISHED SIZE

7½" (19 cm)

SKILL LEVEL

Intermediate

MATERIALS

3 g gold electroplate size 15°
Japanese seed beads (A)

4 g cream 24k gold-lined size 11°
cylinder beads (B)

3 g 24k gold electroplate size 11°
cylinder beads (C)

5 g gold electroplate size 11°
Japanese seed beads (D)

26 crystal golden shadow 2mm
round crystals (E)

2 light Colorado topaz 6mm
round crystals (F)

1 crystal golden shadow
32x17mm marquise crystal stone

Size D nylon beading thread, gold

1 piece 2½" x 2" (6.5 x 5 cm)
backing (heavyweight interfacing
or Lacy's Stiff Stuff)

1 piece 2" x 1½" (5 x 3.8 cm)
Ultrasuede, gold

Toothpicks

Thread conditioner

E-6000 adhesive

TOOLS

Size 12 beading needles

Scissors

TECHNIQUES
YOU WILL USE

BACKSTITCH FOR BEAD
EMBROIDERY (PAGE 13)

EDGING FOR BEAD
EMBROIDERY (PAGE 13)

HERRINGBONE (PAGE 13)

NETTING (PAGE 12)

PEYOTE (PAGE 11)

cat's-eye
BRACELET

Bead embroidery is a great way to bezel unusual-shaped crystals. The large marquise crystal makes a nice focal point for this bracelet in shades of gold.

MARQUISE BEZEL

1 Use a toothpick to spread a thin layer of E-6000 adhesive to the back side of the marquise crystal. Set the crystal in the center of the backing piece and press firmly into place. You can push the backing up around the crystal and hold in place for a little while to help the edges of the crystal to adhere to the backing. You can always go back and use the toothpick to put a dab more glue on the areas that do not stick the first time. Try not to get any glue on the backing outside of the crystal, as it will be hard to sew through when it dries.

2 Put a knot in a 72" (183 cm) piece of thread. Come up from the back alongside the edge of the crystal. String 2D and pass down through the backing at the end of the 2D. Come back up through the backing at the front of the 2D and pass through them again. String 2D and pass down through the backing at the end of the 2D. Come back up through the backing between the first and second beads and pass through the next 3D. Keep adding 2D and coming back up and passing through 3D. This connects the previous group of 2D with the new group of 2D. Work all the way around the crystal. This backstitch row needs to be an even number of beads.

3 String 1D, skip over the next D of the backstitch row, and pass through the next D. Continue working peyote stitch with 1D in each stitch until you have gone all the way around the crystal. Step up into the first D added in this row (**Figure 1, blue thread**).

4 Work 1 more row of peyote stitch with 1A in each stitch (**Figure 1, red thread**).

5 Weave through the beads of the bezel and go down through the backing. Then come back up through the backing close to the bezel and work another row of backstitch following Step 2. This row does not have to be an even number (**Figure 2**).

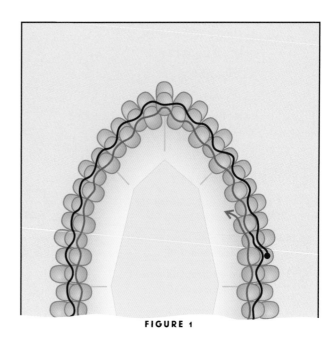

FIGURE 1

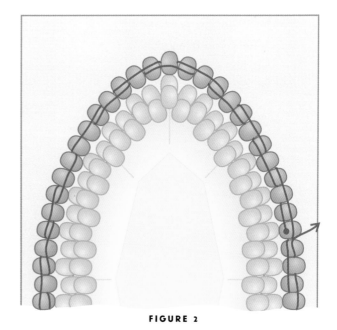

FIGURE 2

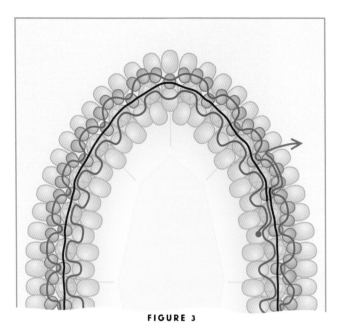

FIGURE 3

FIGURE 4

6 Then weave back up and come out of a D from Step 3. String 1E and pass through the next D from Step 3. The E added should stick out on the side of the bezel. Continue adding Es until you have gone all the way around the crystal. Step up into the first E added in this row (**Figure 3, green thread**).

7 String 1A and pass through the next E from Step 6. Repeat all the way around the crystal. Step up into the first A added in this row (**Figure 3, blue thread**).

8 String 3A and pass through the next A from Step 7. Repeat all the way around the crystal. Weave the thread down through the bezel and tie it off behind the backing (**Figure 3, red thread**).

9 Trim the backing close to the beadwork, making sure not to cut any threads. Make it as neat as possible. Spread a thin layer of E-6000 adhesive on the back of the bead-work with a toothpick. Then place the crystal onto the piece of Ultrasuede. Press down firmly into place. Let the glue dry. Then trim the Ultrasuede to match the backing.

EDGING

10 Anchor 72" (183 cm) of thread in the beadwork and come out at the edge of the Ultrasuede. String 2C; catch the suede about a bead's width over from where the thread originally exited and pass back up through the second C.

11 String 1C; catch the suede about a bead's width over from where the thread originally exited and pass back up through the C just added. Continue all the way around the crystal. After adding the last C, pass down through the first C added in this row, catch the suede, and pass back up through it. This connects the edging at the first and last bead (**Figure 4**).

BAND

12 Find the ten most centered Cs on the side of the crystal. Weave the thread so that it is coming out of the first C of the 10C.

13 String 1C and 1B; pass down through the next C of the edging and pass up through the next C of the edging. Repeat four more times. On the last set, catch the Ultrasuede and pass back up through the same C of the edging; also pass back through the last B (**Figure 5, blue thread**).

14 String 1B and 1C; pass down through the next C from Step 13 and also pass up through the next B from Step 13. This is herringbone stitch. Work herringbone across the rest of the row. After passing down through the last C from Step 13, string 1A and pass back up through the 1C just added. Adding the A at the end is the turnaround for the next row (**Figure 5, red thread**).

15 Keep repeating herringbone, making sure to follow the color pattern; B should stack on B and C should stack on C. Repeat until the band is 5¾" (14.5 cm) long.

16 After adding the last row of the band, pass up and down through the beads of the last two rows to pull the beads closer together (similar to ladder stitch) (**Figure 6**).

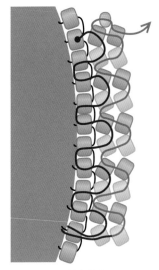

FIGURE 5

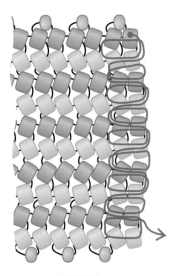

FIGURE 6

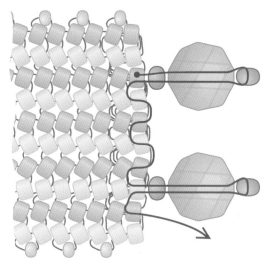

FIGURE 7

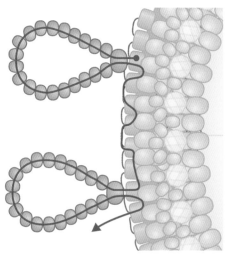

FIGURE 8

BEAD CLASP AND LOOPS

17 Weave the thread so that it is coming out of the third bead at the end of the band, counting in from one side. String 1D, 1F, and 1D. Skip the 1D and pass back through the 1F and 1D and the bead of the band the thread originally exited from. Reinforce.

18 Weave over to the third bead on the end of the band, but counting from the other side. Repeat Step 17 to add another F (**Figure 7**). Reinforce.

19 Find the most centered 7C of the edging row across from the band connection on the other side of the crystal. Anchor 36" (91.5 cm) of thread in the backstitch row and come out of the first C of the centered 7C on the edging. String 1D and enough A to fit comfortably but snugly around the F added in Steps 17–18. Pass back through the 1D and the 1C of the edging. Reinforce.

20 Weave over to the seventh C of the centered 7C and repeat the loop made in Step 19 (**Figure 8**). Reinforce.

swag
NECKLACE

FINISHED SIZE

17½" (44.5 cm)

SKILL LEVEL

Intermediate

MATERIALS

11 g 24k gold-lined size 15°
Japanese seed beads (A)

3 g jet size 15° Japanese seed
beads (B)

2 g cream 24k gold-lined size 11°
cylinder beads (C)

4 g 24k gold-lined size 11°
Japanese seed beads (D)

20 jet 3mm bicone crystals (E)

1 jet 13x6.5mm briolette
crystal drop (F)

1 jet 8mm fire-polished bead (G)

3 jet 12mm crystal rivoli stones

Size D nylon beading thread, gold

Thread conditioner

TOOLS

Size 12 beading needles

Scissors

**TECHNIQUES
YOU WILL USE**

HERRINGBONE (PAGE 13)

PEYOTE (PAGE 11)

A while back, I had made three connected crystal bezels that I intended to use for a bracelet, but the idea just never jelled. I put the piece away in my box where I keep other unused bits and pieces. When I started working on ideas for this book, I pulled out the box and the bezels. I had a sudden inspiration for this necklace and was pleased with the results. So the moral of the story is, save all those bits and pieces of beadwork because one day's failure could be another day's success.

RIVOLI BEZELS

1 With 72" (183 cm) of thread, string 8C. Pass through all 8C again and also pass through the first C again to make a circle (**Figure 1, blue thread**). Leave a 6" (15 cm) tail.

2 String 2C; pass through the next 2C from Step 1. Repeat three more times. After adding the last set of 2C, step up into the first C of the set of 2C added in this row (**Figure 1, red thread**). This sets up the beads for herringbone.

3 String 2C; pass down through the next C from Step 2. String 1A and pass up through the first C of the next set of 2C from Step 2. Repeat three more times. Step up into the first C added in this row (**Figure 2**).

4 String 2C; pass down through the next C from Step 3. String 1A and pass through the next A from Step 3. String 1A and pass up through the next C from Step 3. This is a combination of herringbone and peyote stitch. Repeat three more times. Step up into the first C added in this row (**Figure 3**).

5 String 1D; pass down through the next C from Step 3. String 1A and pass through the next A from Step 4. String 1A and pass through the next A from Step 4. String 1A and pass up through the next C from Step 4. Repeat three more times. Step up into the first D added in this row (**Figure 4**).

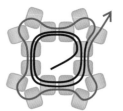

FIGURE 1

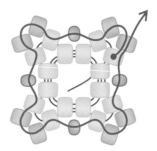

FIGURE 2

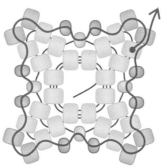

FIGURE 3

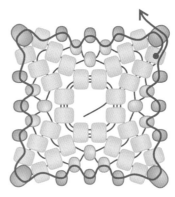

FIGURE 4

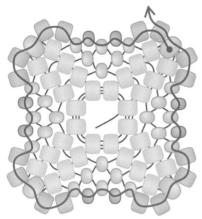

FIGURE 5

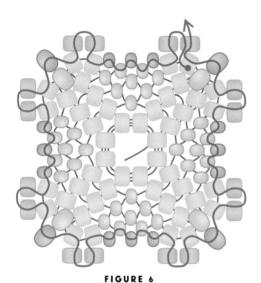

FIGURE 6

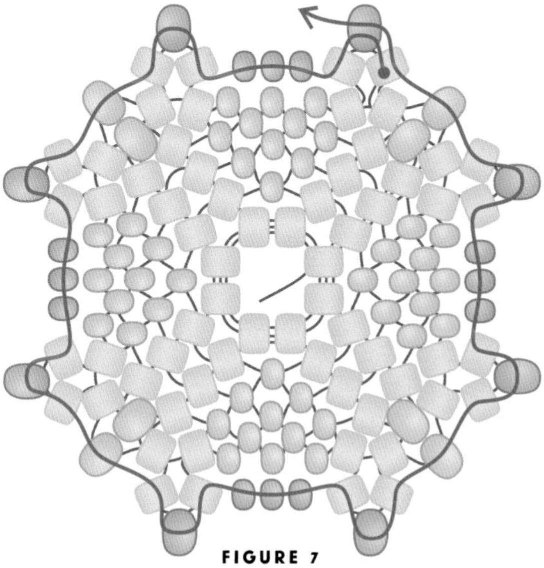

6 String 2C; pass through the next A from Step 5. String 1A and pass through the next A from Step 5. String 1A and pass through the next A from Step 5. String 2C and pass through the next D from Step 5. Repeat three more times. Step up into the first C of the set of 2C added in this row (**Figure 5**).

7 String 2C; pass down through the next C from Step 6. String 1A and pass through the next A from Step 6. String 1A and pass through the next A from Step 6. String 1A and pass up through the next C from Step 6. String 2C and pass down through the next C from Step 6. String 1D and pass through the first C of the next set of 2C from Step 6. Repeat three more times. Step up into the first C of the set of 2C added in this row (**Figure 6**).

8 String 1D and pass down through the next C from Step 7. String 3A and pass up through the next C of the next set of 2C from Step 7. String 1D; pass down through the next C and also pass through the next D and the next C of the next set of 2C. Pull snug. The beadwork will start to cup up a little at this point. Repeat three more times. Step up into the first D added in this row (**Figure 7**).

FIGURE 7

9 String 3A and pass through the next D added in Step 8. Pull snug. Repeat seven more times (there were 8D added in Step 8 and there will be 3A added in between them in this row). Insert one of the 12mm rivolis and pull snug (**Figure 8**). Reinforce this row.

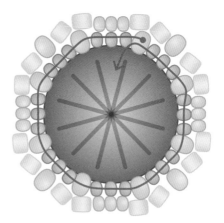

FIGURE 8

10 Weave the thread so that it is coming out of a 1D before a set of 3A that were added in Step 8. String 1A, 1E, and 1A; pass through the next 1D, 3A, and 1D. Repeat three more times. Pull snug (**Figure 9**).

11 Make 2 more rivoli bezels following Steps 1–10.

CONNECTIONS

12 Weave a thread on a bezel so that it is coming out of a 1A after a 1E from Step 10. String 1E and pass through the 1A, 1E, and 1A on another bezel. Weave through the beads and come out of the next 1A after the next 1E. String 1E and pass through the next 1A, 1E, and 1A on the third bezel. Weave over to the other side and repeat (**Figure 10, blue thread**).

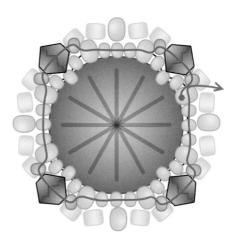

FIGURE 9

13 Weave the thread so that it is coming out of the middle A of the 3A on the middle bezel that is directly across from one of the other bezels. String 1E and pass through the middle A of the 3A on the end bezel. Pass back through the 1E and also pass through the 1A the thread originally exited from. Weave over to the other 3A on the other side of the middle bezel and repeat (**Figure 10, red thread**).

FIGURE 10

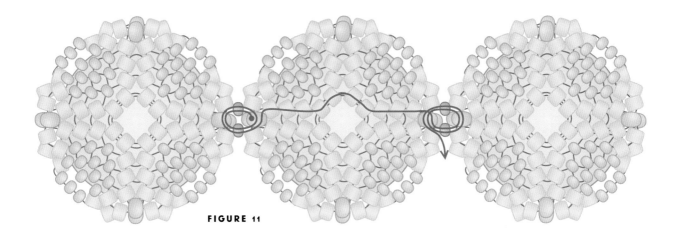

FIGURE 11

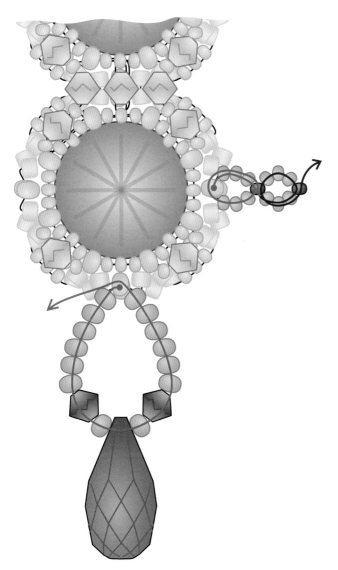

FIGURE 12

14 Weave the thread on the back side of the middle bezel so that it is coming out of the 1D from Step 5 that is across from one of the end bezels. String 1A, pass through the 1D of the end bezel; string 1A and pass through the 1D the thread originally exited from. Reinforce one more time. Weave over to the 1D on the other side of the middle bezel and repeat (**Figure 11**).

FRINGE

15 Weave the thread on an end bezel so that it is coming out of the 1D on an end bezel from Step 7 that is across from the bezel connections. String 6D, 1E, 1D, 1F, 1D, 1E, and 6D and pass through the 1D the thread originally exited from (**Figure 12, red thread**).

CHAINS

16 Weave a new 72" (183 cm) length of thread so that it is coming out of the 1D from Step 7 on a side of the end bezel with the fringe. String 3A, 1B, and 3A; pass through the 1D the thread originally exited from and also pass through the first 3A and the 1B (**Figure 12, green thread**).

17 String 3A, 1B, and 3A; pass through the 1B the thread originally exited from and also pass through the first 3A and the 1B (**Figure 12, blue thread**). Repeat until there are 62 circles. Then repeat Steps 16–17 on the other 1D on the other side of the bezel.

18 Repeat Steps 16–17 on the middle bezel, but repeat for a total of 54 circles.

19 Repeat Steps 16–17 on the top bezel, without the fringe, but repeat for a total of 48 circles.

ENDS, CLASP BEAD, AND LOOP

20 The thread on the end circle of the top chain (48 loops) should be coming out of the 1B at the end going toward the other chains. String 1D and pass through the 1B on the end circle of the middle chain. String 1D and pass through the 1B on the bottom chain. (Make sure that none of the chains are twisted.) String 3D and then pass through the 1B, 1D, 1B, 1D, 1B, and the 3D again. Reinforce one more time. End with the thread coming out of the 3D (**Figure 13, blue thread**).

21 String 4D, 1G, and 3D. Skip the 3D and pass back through the 1G and the next 1D. String 3D and then pass through the 3D the thread originally exited (**Figure 13, red thread**). Reinforce.

22 Repeat Step 20 on the other 3 chains on the other side of the bezels (**Figure 14, blue thread**). String enough D to fit comfortably but snugly around the 1G (**Figure 14, red thread**). Reinforce.

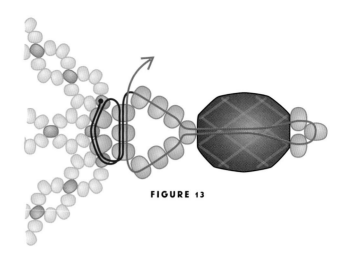

FIGURE 13

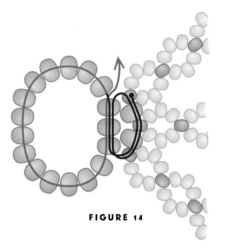

FIGURE 14

FINISHED SIZE

16½" (42 cm)

SKILL LEVEL

Intermediate

MATERIALS

24 g topaz raspberry gold luster size 15° Japanese seed beads (A)

10 g gold electroplate size 15° Japanese seed beads (B)

6 g topaz rose gold luster size 11° Japanese seed beads (C)

40 g gold electroplate gold size 11° Japanese seed beads (D)

348 purple velvet 2mm glass pearls (E)

200 bright gold 3mm glass pearls (F)

9 amethyst 12mm crystal rivoli stones (G)

11 amethyst 18mm crystal rivoli stones (H)

1 amethyst 8mm fire-polished bead (I)

2 amethyst/gold 44mm pure crystal drops (J)

Size D nylon beading thread, gold

Thread conditioner

TOOLS

Size 12 beading needles

Scissors

TECHNIQUES YOU WILL USE

NETTING (PAGE 12)

PEYOTE (PAGE 11)

gala
NECKLACE

This necklace is a bit over the top. I wanted to make a really lush, ornate necklace, and I think this fits the bill. You could always make just one of the strands if you wanted a simpler silhouette. Both the large and small bezels have a double layer, which gives the necklace a lot of great dimension. The small bezels with a smaller pure crystal drop would make great earrings.

LARGE BEZEL

1 With 90" (228.5 cm) of thread, string 12A. Pass through all 12A again and also pass through the first A again to make a small circle. Leave an 8" (20.5 cm) tail (**Figure 1, turquoise thread**).

2 String 3A, skip over the next A from Step 1, and pass through the next A. Repeat five more times. Step up into the first 2A added in this row (**Figure 1, orange thread**).

3 String 5A; pass through the middle bead of the next set of 3A from Step 2. Repeat five more times. Step up into the first 3A added in this row (**Figure 1, green thread**).

4 String 7A; pass through the middle bead of the next set of 5A from Step 3. Repeat five more times. Step up into the first 4A added in this row (**Figure 1, blue thread**).

5 String 9A; pass through the middle bead of the next set of 7A from Step 4. Repeat five more times. Step up into the first 5A added in this row (**Figure 1, red thread**).

6 String 9A; pass through the middle bead of the next set of 9A from Step 5. Pull snug. Repeat five more times. Step up into the first 5A added in this row. This row will start to cup up a little. Place 1H into the bead-work, right side facing up. Hold it in place as you work the next row.

7 String 7A; pass through the middle bead of the next set of 9A from Step 6. Pull snug. Repeat five more times (**Figure 2**). Reinforce this row one more time.

8 Weave the thread so that it is coming out of the fifth A from the row of 9A from Step 6. String 1D, 1F, and 1D; pass through the next fifth A from the row of 9A from Step 6. Repeat five more times. After adding the last set, weave down and come out of the fifth A from the row of 9A from Step 5 (**Figure 3**).

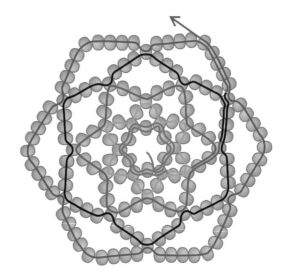

FIGURE 1

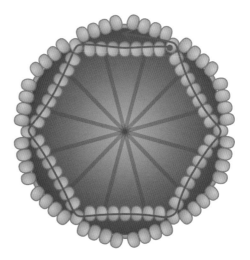

FIGURE 2

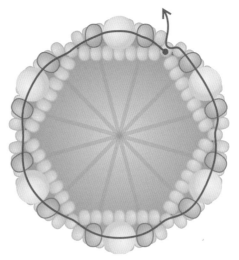

FIGURE 3

FIGURE 4

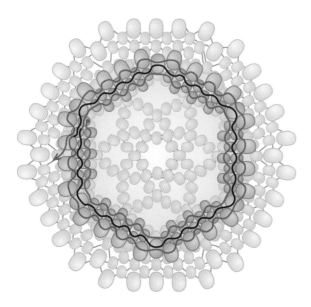

FIGURE 5

FIGURE 6

9 String 9A and pass through the next fifth A from the row of 9A from Step 5. Repeat five more times. After adding the last set, step up into the first A of the first set of 9A (**Figure 4, orange thread**).

10 String 1A, skip over the next A from Step 9, and pass through the next A (peyote stitch). Repeat three more times. String 1D and pass through the first A of the next set of 9A from Step 9. Repeat this sequence five more times. After adding the last set, step up into the first A added in this row (**Figure 4, green thread**).

11 Work a row of peyote stitch with 1D in each stitch for a total of 30D in this row (**Figure 4, blue thread**).

12 Weave the thread so that it is coming out of a fourth bead of the row of 7A from Step 4 (**Figure 4, red thread**). String 7A and pass through the next fourth A of the row of 7A from Step 4. Repeat five more times. Step up into the first A of the first set of 7A added in this row (**Figure 5, green thread**).

13 String 1A, skip over the next A from Step 12, and pass through the next one (peyote stitch). Repeat two more times. String 1D and pass through the first A of the next set of 7A from Step 12. Repeat this sequence five more times. After adding the last set, step up into the first A added in this row (**Figure 5, blue thread**).

14 Work a row of peyote stitch with 1D in each stitch for a total of 24D in this row. Step up into the first D added in this row (**Figure 5, red thread**).

15 Repeat Step 14 for another row of peyote stitch with 24D (**Figure 6, green thread**).

16 Work a row of peyote stitch with 1C in each stitch for a total of 24C in this row. Step up into the first C added in this row (**Figure 6, blue thread**).

17 Repeat Step 14 for another row of peyote stitch with 24D (**Figure 6, red thread**).

18 String 1E and pass through the next D from Step 17. String 1F and pass through the next D from Step 17. Repeat for a row of peyote stitch that alternates a 1E with a 1F in the stitches. Step up into the first E added in this row (**Figure 7, green thread**).

19 Work a row of peyote stitch with 1D in each stitch for a total of 24D in this row. Step up into the first D added in this row (**Figure 7, blue thread**).

20 The thread should be coming out of a 1D before a 1F. String 4B and pass through the next D from Step 19. String 2B and pass through the next D from Step 19. Repeat around, adding 4B over the 1F and 2B over the 1E from Step 18, passing through the 1D from Step 19 (**Figure 7, red thread**). Weave in and tie off the tail thread.

21 Make 10 more large bezels following Steps 1–20.

SMALL BEZEL

22 With 72" (183 cm) of thread, string 12A. Pass through all 12A again and also pass through the first A again to make a small circle (**Figure 8, orange thread**). Leave an 8" (20.5 cm) tail.

23 String 3A, skip over the next A from Step 22, and pass through the next A. Repeat five more times. Step up into the first 2A added in this row (**Figure 8, green thread**).

24 String 5A; pass through the middle bead of the next set of 3A from Step 23. Repeat five more times. Step up into the first 3A added in this row (**Figure 8, blue thread**).

25 String 7A; pass through the middle bead of the next set of 5A from Step 24. Repeat five more times. Step up into the first 4A added in this row (**Figure 8, red thread**).

26 String 1D, 1E, and 1D; pass through the middle bead of the next set of 7A from Step 25. Repeat five more times. Insert 1G, right side facing up. Pull snug and reinforce (**Figure 9**).

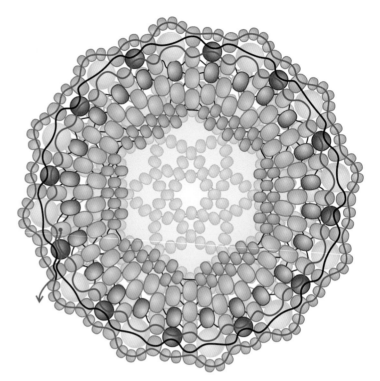

FIGURE 7

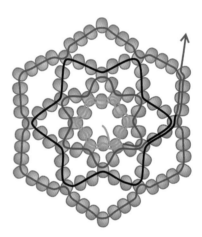

FIGURE 8

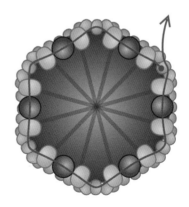

FIGURE 9

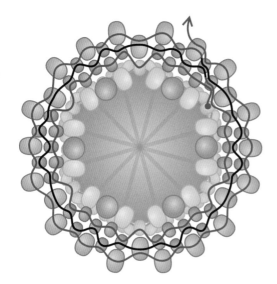

FIGURE 10

FIGURE 11

27 Weave the thread so that it is coming out of the fourth A of a set of 7A from Step 25. String 5A and pass through the next fourth A of the next set of 7A from Step 25. Repeat five times. Step up into the first A of the first set of 5A added in this row (**Figure 10, green thread**).

28 String 1A, skip over the next A from Step 27, and pass through the next one. Repeat one more time. String 1D and pass through the first A from the next set of 5A from Step 27. Repeat this sequence five more times. Step up into the first A added in this row (**Figure 10, blue thread**).

29 Work a row of peyote stitch with 1D in each stitch for a total of 18D in this row (**Figure 10, red thread**).

30 Weave the thread so that it is coming out of the third A of a set of 5A from Step 24. String 5A and pass through the next third A of the set of 5A from Step 24. Repeat five more times. Step up into the first A of the first set of 5A added in this row (**Figure 11, turquoise thread**).

31 String 1A, skip over the next A from Step 30, and pass through the next one. Repeat one more time. String 1D and pass through the first A from the next set of 5A from Step 30. Repeat this sequence five more times. Step up into the first A added in this row (**Figure 11, orange thread**).

32 Work a row of peyote stitch with 1D in each stitch for a total of 18D in this row. Step up into the first D added in this row (**Figure 11, green thread**).

33 Work a row of peyote stitch with 1C in each stitch for a total of 18C in this row. Step up into the first C added in this row (**Figure 11, blue thread**).

34 Repeat Step 32 for another row of peyote stitch with 18D in each stitch (**Figure 11, red thread**).

35 Work a row of peyote stitch with 1E in each stitch for a total of 18E in this row. Step up into the first E added in this row (**Figure 12, green thread**).

36 Repeat Step 32 for another row of peyote stitch with 18D in each stitch (**Figure 12, blue thread**).

37 String 3B and pass through the next D from Step 36. Repeat, adding 18 sets of 3B (**Figure 12, red thread**). Weave in and tie off the tail thread.

38 Make 8 more small bezels following Steps 22–37.

LARGE BEZEL CONNECTIONS

39 Weave a thread on a large bezel so that it is coming out of the middle 2B, on a row from Step 20, that are over a 1F added in Step 18. Pass through the middle 2B on another large bezel that are over a 1F from Step 18. Pass through the 2B the thread originally exited from and weave down to the next 2B that are over a 1E from Step 18. Pass through a 2B over a 1E from Step 18 on the second bezel. Pass through the 2B the thread originally exited from and weave down to the next middle 2B that are over the next 1F from Step 18. Pass through the middle 2B on the second bezel on the next middle 2B that are over a 1F from Step 18. Pass through the 2B the thread originally exited from (**Figure 13**).

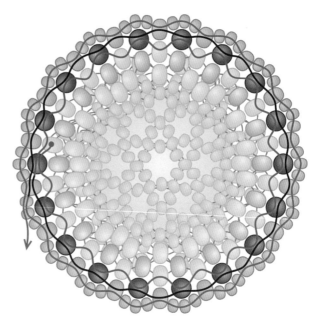

FIGURE 12

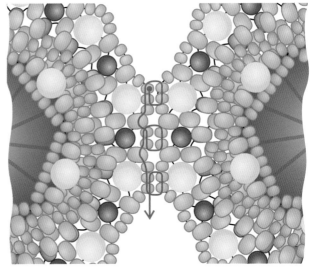

FIGURE 13

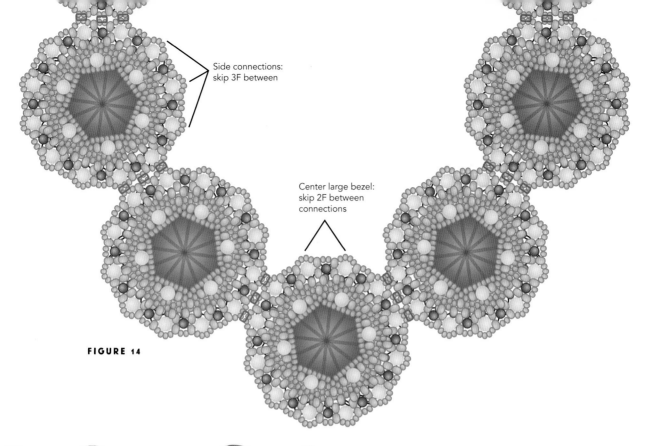

Side connections:
skip 3F between

Center large bezel:
skip 2F between
connections

FIGURE 14

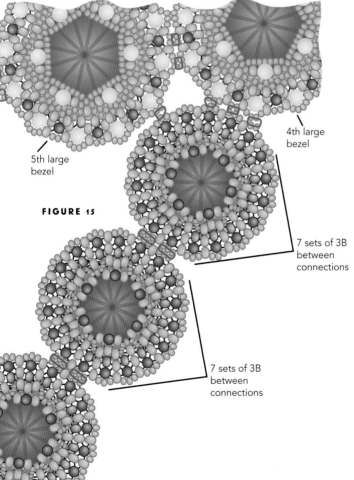

FIGURE 15

5th large
bezel

4th large
bezel

7 sets of 3B
between
connections

7 sets of 3B
between
connections

40 Connect all the large bezels following Step 39. **Figure 14** illustrates where the connections are made on the bezels.

SMALL BEZEL CONNECTIONS

41 **Figure 15** illustrates where to connect a small bezel to the fourth and fifth large bezel, counting in from the end. It is connected in three places with the B added in the last rows on both bezels. On the large bezels, it is connected at the middle 2B, and on the small bezels, it is connected at the middle B in the same way as the connections in Step 39.

42 Connect a second small bezel to the first small bezel connected in Step 41. Figure 15 illustrates the placement of the connections.

43 Connect 3 more small bezels. Figure 15 illustrates the placement of the connections.

44 Following Steps 41–43, connect 4 more small bezels to the fourth and fifth large bezels, counting in from the other side.

45 Connect the 2 strips of small bezels together. **Figure 16** illustrates the placement.

DROPS

46 Weave a thread so that it is coming out of the 2B on the center large bezel that are below the fourth E, counting away from the connections. String 3B, 1J, and 3B; pass through the 2B the thread originally exited from on the opposite side (**Figure 17**). Reinforce.

47 Weave a thread so that it is coming out of the 1B of the center small bezel that is below the sixth E, counting away from the connections. String 3B, 1J, and 3B; pass through the 1B the thread originally exited from on the opposite side. Reinforce.

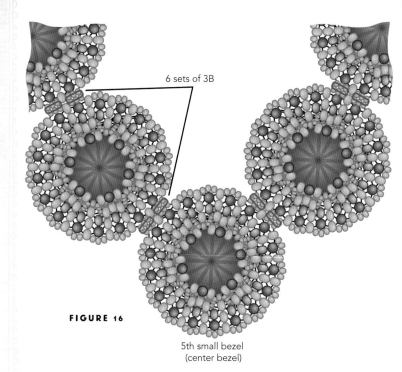

6 sets of 3B

FIGURE 16

5th small bezel
(center bezel)

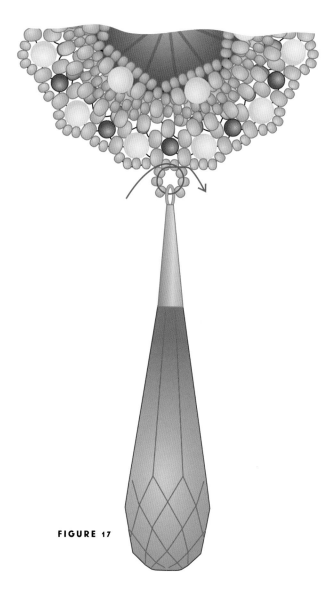

FIGURE 17

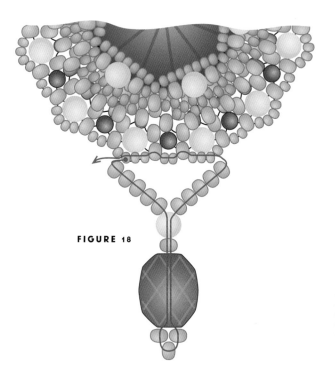

FIGURE 18

CLASP BEAD AND LOOP

48 Weave a thread so that it is coming out of the third B across from the connections on an end large bezel. String 5D, 1F, 1D, 1I, and 3D. Skip the last 3D and pass back through the 1I, 1D, and 1F. String 5D and pass through the third B of the next set of 3B next to the set the thread originally exited from (**Figure 18**). Reinforce.

49 Weave a thread on the other end large bezel so that it is coming out of the third B across from the connections. String 5D, 1F, and enough D to fit comfortably but snugly around the 1I. Pass back through the 1F. String 5D and pass through the third B of the next set of 3B next to the set the thread originally exited from (**Figure 19**). Reinforce.

FIGURE 19

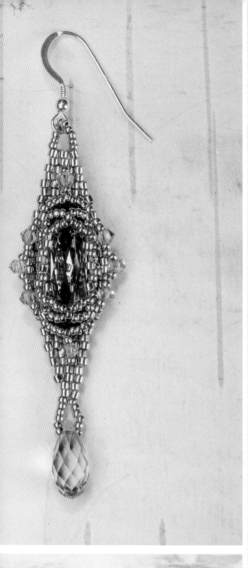

resources

The materials used to create the projects in this book can be found at your local bead or craft store or favorite online retailer. Below are the sources for the materials I used to make the projects.

Artbeads.com
artbeads.com

Beyond Beadery
PO Box 460
Rollinsville, CO 80474
beyondbeadery.com

Fire Mountain Gems and Beads
1 Fire Mountain Way
Grants Pass, OR 97526
firemountaingems.com

Fusion Beads
3830 Stone Way N
Seattle, WA 98103
fusionbeads.com

Rio Grande
7500 Bluewater Road NW
Albuquerque, NM 87121
riogrande.com

INDEX

20   19   18   17   16   5   4   3   2   1

a content + ecommerce company

Distributed in Canada by Fraser Direct
100 Armstrong Avenue
Georgetown, ON, Canada L7G 5S4
Tel: (905) 877-4411

Distributed in the U.K. and Europe by F&W MEDIA INTERNATIONAL
Brunel House, Newton Abbot, Devon, TQ12 4PU, England
Tel: (+44) 1626 323200, Fax: (+44) 1626 323319
E-mail: enquiries@fwmedia.com

SRN: 16BD05
ISBN-13: 978-1-63250-352-7

PDF SRN: EP12710
PDF ISBN-13: 978-1-63250-383-1

EDITED BY Christine Doyle

DESIGNED BY Karla Baker

TECHNICAL EDIT BY Bonnie Brooks

PHOTOGRAPHY BY Jack Deutsch

ILLUSTRATIONS BY Bonnie Brooks

about the author

Kelly Wiese is the author of two books, *A Beaded Romance* and *Beaded Allure*. She was a 2011 *Beadwork* Magazine Designer of the Year. Kelly loves to use size 15 seed beads (her motto is "the smaller the better") and crystals in her work, which is often described as romantic and delicate. She resides with her husband, three dogs, and six cats in Colorado, where she spends as much time as possible playing with beads. Visit her website at www.beadparlor.com.

METRIC CONVERSION CHART

To convert	to	multiply by
Inches	Centimeters	2.54
Centimeters	Inches	0.4
Feet	Centimeters	30.5
Centimeters	Feet	0.03
Yards	Meters	0.9
Meters	Yards	1.1

dedication

To my husband, Paul,
thank you for all your
love and support.

You made this possible.

acknowledgments

My parents have always supported my creative endeavors. Growing up, I had an artist's easel, a pottery wheel, a sewing machine, and any number of craft kits given to me as presents. I treasured all these things and am very grateful that my parents felt this was an important part of my education. Being encouraged to create is what eventually led me to the wonderful world of beading. Once I discovered it, there was no turning back!

I have made so many wonderful friends through beading, and they continue to be such a comfort and joy to me. Thank you to my show buddy Virginia who has done more shows with me than I can count. She has been there for the good, bad, and everything in between.

My husband has been so supportive through yet another book process. I could not imagine going through it all without him by my side. I love working from my home studio with all my furbabies to keep me company and my husband to keep me sane.

I am thrilled to be working with all the wonderful people at Interweave for this book. Thank you to Kerry Bogert for all her help in making this third book a reality. Also special thanks go to Melinda Barta who years ago encouraged me to submit several designs to *Beadwork* magazine and to Jean Campbell for encouraging me to try new things such as making DVDs. You have all helped me grow and learn, and I am forever grateful.